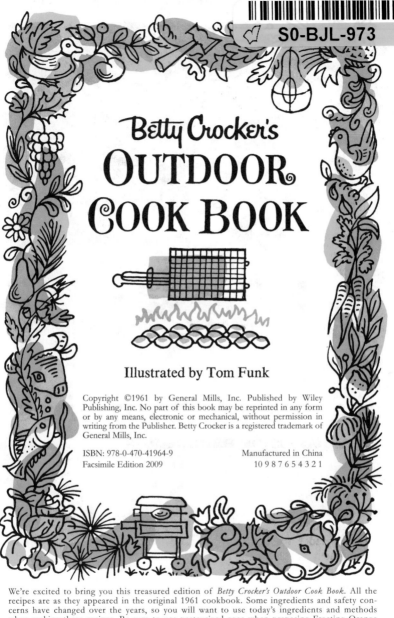

Betty Crocker's OUTDOOR COOK BOOK

Illustrated by Tom Funk

Copyright ©1961 by General Mills, Inc. Published by Wiley Publishing, Inc. No part of this book may be reprinted in any form or by any means, electronic or mechanical, without permission in writing from the Publisher. Betty Crocker is a registered trademark of General Mills, Inc.

ISBN: 978-0-470-41964-9

Facsimile Edition 2009

Manufactured in China

10 9 8 7 6 5 4 3 2 1

We're excited to bring you this treasured edition of *Betty Crocker's Outdoor Cook Book*. All the recipes are as they appeared in the original 1961 cookbook. Some ingredients and safety concerns have changed over the years, so you will want to use today's ingredients and methods when making these recipes. Be sure to use pasteurized eggs when preparing Frosting Orange Nog (page 46) and Caesar Salad (page 133). Also follow today's grilling and outdoor cooking safety guidelines.

WILEY

TABLE OF CONTENTS

Dear Friend,

Who doesn't love to eat outdoors? The tantalizing aroma of sizzling chicken or steaks, the mellow glow of the coals, the hum of happy voices—it all adds up to fun for everyone. And the setting can be porch, patio, park, seashore, or stream.

In this book you'll find many interesting recipes and ideas, developed for outdoor cooking and dining. And you'll find them divided into three major sections: first, the basics of barbecuing—the fire, the fuel and heat control; second, occasions for outdoor feasts—Backyard or Terrace Barbecues, Shore Cooking, Seaside in the Backyard, Cooking Afloat, Cruising on Land, Packtrip Cooking, Breakfast Cookouts, and Picnics; and third, a collection of recipes for outdoor dining—from the simplest to the most exotic fare. These recipes include everything you might like to cook or eat outdoors—meats and main dishes, vegetables, fruits, salads, breads, and desserts.

We hope you'll turn to this book often for help in planning for dining *al fresco*. It will be as delightful and as exciting as any meal served indoors.

Cordially,

Betty Crocker

THE BASICS OF BARBECUING

A striking change is taking place in American cooking and entertaining. The backyard barbecue is fast becoming the nation's number one hobby as, each year, more families discover that fun and good fellowship seem to double around an open fire; that nothing is more appetizing than the aroma of food grilling over glowing coals; and that the easy informality of service under the wide sky makes even the most elaborate patio party seem carefree.

The taste of charcoal broiled meats is so delicious that many of us no longer let the end of summer mean good-bye to the "Cook-out." When the snow flies, it becomes the "Cook-in" at the fireplace or at the broiling hearth now so often seen as a feature of new kitchens or family rooms.

Call it barbecue, steak fry, patio party, hot dog roast, or cookout— it is one of the best ways to entertain two or twenty, once you have learned the basic rules for successful cooking and serving outside.

THE FIRE

Magnificent meals may be cooked out of doors with equipment as simple as a grid from the oven propped on bricks. And the most elaborate and expensive gear can produce a dismal failure—if the fire is not right.

Therefore, the first and most important rule for success is "Understand Your Fire."

This means learning how to choose the best location, equipment, and fuel for your particular purpose and turning their special advantages and limitations to fullest account.

Many beginners take it for granted that the delicious flavor of barbecued food comes from the smoke of a newly kindled fire. This is not so. That first smoke leaves no more than the acrid taste of charring fiber, not the true smoky seasoning that makes even the plainest of foods such a gourmet's delight.

That savory taste of smoke comes from the delicate charring of food in contact with a very high smokeless heat. There are several good ways to arrive at an emphatic smoky seasoning. Flare-ups should be sternly controlled during grilling. A pungent smoke taste is achieved by adding commercially packed hickory pellets or chips, or well-soaked sawdust

or bits of hardwood to a bed of evenly glowing coals. Soak hickory chips in water 2 to 3 hours, then place under, on, or in center of hot coals so hickory smoke will flavor meat. This can be a tricky method for the novice, so many prefer to sprinkle meats or fish with smoke-flavored salt, or to use a few drops of a liquid smoke seasoning in a basting sauce. Small branches of green bay leaves tossed on for a final crackling flare add a distinctive taste. If you have a flourishing herb garden, try handfuls of freshly picked and washed thyme, marjoram, or basil for a delightful difference.

No fire is ready for grilling until it has reduced itself to bright coals glowing with even smokeless color and heat.

The first leaping flames of a wood fire look powerful, but their heat dances away in the air, scorching the outside of food while barely warming the interior, and frequently leaving a sad smear of greasy soot, ruinous to the appearance of light-colored food.

Grilling over briquets can also be a problem if the food is placed over the fire before the briquets are ash-grey. If some areas of black show, the heat will be too low for best results. Steaks, especially, are less than perfect if started over too low a heat. Their juices drip and are wasted, and they come off a slow fire steamed and grey through instead of sizzling brown outside and temptingly pink within.

Each fire you kindle behaves differently, even if you use the same kind of fuel in the same location. The direction of the wind, its strength, air temperature, its degree of humidity, a handful more or less of fuel, and the way you heap up or rake out the coals—all of these influence the fire's character and performance.

The basic rules for fire building and control that follow will give you a fast start in the right direction, but only by firsthand experience does anyone develop that second sense that tells the expert how to make the outdoor grill produce reliable results.

Rule One: Before you light your fire, collect or have easily at hand *all* of the fuel you expect to use—and a little more!

Rule Two: Once your pilot fire is kindled and burning well, add as readily as possible *all* of the rest of the fuel so that it can burn down all at once to an even bed of coals.

Rule Three: Use a little more fuel than actually necessary. Nothing is a wider open invitation to trouble than a fire that is too small.

Rule Four: When necessary to add fuel to a well-established fire—as it sometimes is during a long cooking period—add it at the edges and rake it in when well kindled. Never put the fresh fuel in the center as this reduces heat rapidly.

Rule Five: Allow plenty of time for the fire to reach its proper cooking heat. Half an hour is the minimum for charcoal briquets, and 45 minutes to an hour is safer.

Rule Six: Once your fire is well under way, disturb it as little as possible. Constant poking and raking breaks up pockets of heat and lowers temperature.

Rule Seven: Develop some stern method of kibitzer control. People who would not dream of regulating your kitchen oven seem unable to resist "helping" the outdoor chef by stirring up his fire. They mean well. Indeed, such activity usually shows the first gleam of determination to try outdoor cooking for themselves. But threaten them off with the tongs, if necessary. Two firemasters is one too many.

Fuels

Note: All recipes in this book were tested with charcoal briquets. Therefore, chefs using wood as fuel should use tests for doneness as their guide rather than cooking time.

Wood is the classic fuel of campers and is still the favorite of many backyard and fireplace barbecuers. The most suitable woods for grilling are hard ones such as oak, birch, ash, maple, fruit, and nut woods among others. Hard woods produce hot, long-burning coals and an even heat. Soft woods are good for kindling only. They burn away too quickly to produce the essential bed of evenly glowing charcoal.

Avoid any resinous woods. Pine leaves a strong turpentine taste. Cedar, fir, and spruce add a biting medicated flavor most unpleasant

to many people. Eucalyptus smoke has an enchanting aroma, but don't be tempted unless you want your meal to taste like cough drops.

Charcoal is by far the most popular fuel today because it comes in compact units, easy to transport or store. It produces a bed of bright coals more reliably and quickly than do logs or driftwood — and without the hazard of flying sparks.

Charcoal comes in two forms, lump and briquets, each with its special advantage. Lump charcoal works well in a hibachi for the quick grilling of fast-cooking foods such as small steaks, chops, hamburgers, and fish fillets. Since lump or stick charcoal may be broken in small pieces and is less compressed than briquets, it can reach grilling heat faster. By the same token it burns away faster. Therefore, for foods that take longer cooking, such as roasted potatoes or meats, briquets are the better choice.

There is quite a wide variation in the performance of charcoal briquets. Some brands kindle more slowly than others. Some, such as those made from fruit pits, produce more heat than do those made from woods. It is a good idea to experiment with several brands, find one that gives you dependable results, and stay with it. There are enough surprises in outdoor cooking without adding any unnecessary ones of your own.

Properly used, briquets are not expensive. A few experiments will teach you that you need decidedly less fuel than you imagine. Many cooks, new to open fire techniques, cover the entire firebowl of a brazier or grill with briquets heaped three deep and so produce a fire that is far too hot and that will burn on long after dinner is eaten and guests have gone home. On the other hand, nothing is more defeating than a fire that is so meager that it leaves the outer edges of food underdone. One of my friends, who charcoal grills summer and winter, suggests starting with 20 to 25 briquets when grilling just one food. It is far wiser to use a little more fuel than necessary than a little less since briquets can be doused in a bucket of water and reused if given time to dry out thoroughly.

Charcoal may be lighted with paper and wood kindling placed under a cone-shaped heap of briquets or lumps. Briquets have a tendency to ignite slowly, however, so most people who do a lot of outdoor cooking find that a liquid starter makes life simpler.

Whichever method of fire starting you choose, the charcoal fire is best laid in a tepee or cone shape to start. Don't be dismayed if nothing seems to be happening after the kindling burns away and the briquets sit there, cold and stubbornly black except for a few small spots of whitish grey. These small areas of ash mean that the fire is burning quietly toward the heart, and all is well. Never add more starter fluid after the fire has started. Busy yourself with trimming steak, skewering kabobs, or wrapping vegetables in foil. After 10 or 15 minutes you can begin to turn the briquets with widely spreading ash so that they aid others to catch. Within another half hour, when all are going strongly red, spread them out to cover the area you need, and then leave alone as much as possible

All fires need a draft. If you are using a shallow firebowl, the normal flow of light breeze will provide enough draft, though briquets kindle much more willingly if there is a draft door you can open in the bottom of the brazier. If you are using a deep bowl without a draft door, build the fire on several inches of coarse gravel, or a commercial product made for lining fire boxes, so that air has a chance to reach the fire and feed it oxygen from below. After several usings, gravel should be washed in hot water to clean it of greasy drippings. Be sure to dry it thoroughly before using it again. A moisture-soaked piece of gravel may explode, and the flying fragments can inflict stinging wounds.

Store all charcoal in a dry place between usings. It absorbs moisture from the air readily and kindles slowly when damp.

Coal briquets make a fine fire but they are used less often than charcoal ones, mainly because they are a bit more smudgy to handle. Packagers have found an answer to this problem. Briquets of all kinds are to be had in heavy bags or cartons complete with starter. All you need to do is put the clean package on your fireplace and light one match. This makes transportation of fuel to a picnic site neat and easy. But fuel in such small quantities naturally is far more expensive than that in the more practical 50 or 100 pound sacks.

Bottled and canned fuels are for use in camp stoves only. These include propane, alcohol, and solidified canned heat. Such fuels are not suitable for grilling; they are only used for pot and pan cooking. Camp stoves are of great convenience to the station-wagon camper since they can produce hot foods with the least delay and may be used in many sites where open fires are prohibited. But the food they produce is no different in taste from that prepared on the range at home.

Fire Starters

Kindling offers no great problem in dry weather. A few brittle twigs and small sticks set tepee shape over a few balls of crumpled newspaper, and you are in business. If no kindling is available, "Cape Cod Logs" are a good substitute. They are made by opening three sheets of newspaper, stacking them, rolling diagonally from one corner to the opposite one, and tying the resulting wand in a firm knot.

*Liquid starters** are a time saver, especially with briquets. A little

goes a long way, but those who do a great deal of outdoor cooking find it more economical to use an odorless paint thinner. Your dealer will recommend the right one if you tell him that you need it for a fire starter.

Do not use kerosene. The odor is apt to linger in your fire bed. Even a few unburned drops can give your luscious food a strong unpleasant taste.

Never use gasoline for a starter. It is much too dangerous around any open fire. Special precautions should be taken with any starter fluid. Once the fire is going, place container of liquid at a safe distance from the fire.

Half a cup of liquid starter is sufficient to kindle a medium-sized fire. Dribble it on slowly so that it soaks into the fuel rather than running off into the fire bed. Let it stand for 3 or 4 minutes. Then touch it in several places with a lighted match.

An even better idea is to keep a small supply of especially prepared briquets on hand in an empty coffee can or any other metal container

*NOTE: Use only a barbecue starter fluid and never any other flammable liquid to start a fire based on today's grilling safety knowledge.

with a tight lid. Fill the can with briquets. Cover them with liquid starter. Let them soak for an hour. One or two will get a sizable fire off to a fast start. These can be kept indefinitely in a tightly sealed can. Don't use a glass jar! It is too easy for a child or a romping dog to knock over and possibly turn a whole terrace or lawn into a roaring fire bed.

A third method is to cut both ends out of a large tin can. Place in center of fire box, fill with charcoal, pour on starter fluid, and light. This small area will start more quickly. Then remove can and fire will spread to other briquets.

Solid starters are easy to transport without fear of leakage. They are available in flake or stick form. The semi-solid ones in cans that squirt out foam under pressure are also effective.

Electric starters are neat and practical if there is an electric outlet handy. Many of the more elaborate barbecue units designed for terrace cooking come with starter coils built in. Separate units are available for use in simpler barbecue grills or braziers or in fireplaces.

Locating the Fire

All fires are going to give off some smoke, and more than one party has been ruined by remembering this basic law of cause and effect a little too late.

In the woods or on the shore, take a few minutes to make sure the breeze will blow smoke away from, not toward, the site you have chosen for eating.

Be careful to build the fire downwind from tent, car, table, and other hard-to-move gear, and at a safe distance from shrubs, trees, or dry grass that could be ignited by flying sparks.

When cooking on a terrace or in the backyard, set up the tables farther from your cooking area than you think really necessary so that a small change of wind will not flavor your guests as well as your food with smoke.

Heat Control

Each time you build a fire, many different factors need to be considered. Any fire burns faster in a strong draft, but you may need to allow more cooking time since heat is carried away faster in a brisk wind. Humidity affects the fire; so does the degree of dryness of fuel, wind direction as well as force, and the size and shape of your fire. The expert turns all of these elements to account. Controlling the heat of an outdoor fire takes real skill, but a little practice will soon show you how to lower or raise the fire's heat efficiently by use of the following methods.

Windbreaks are great aids in varying the draft and in reflecting heat. Metal hoods and sliding collars are built-in parts of many units. It is entirely unnecessary to depend on expensive equipment, however. A strip of curved tin can be rigged easily and moved at will to accomplish the same purpose. A wide strip of foil held in place by sticks makes an easily portable windbreak for the campfire.

Dampers, or draft doors, are an integral part of hibachis, cooking kettles, many wheeled barbecue units, and most stationary fireplaces. Such dampers are a great help, opened wide, in getting a fire off to a fast start. Almost shut, they maintain the lower, steady heat needed for long cooking. Half open, they bring up the heat for the faster grilling required by steaks, chops, and hamburgers.

Ash builds up in a grey layer as briquets burn. Under most circumstances this ash need be of no concern to the cook since it gradually flakes off by itself. However, if ash is gently knocked off without disturbing the shape of the fire, the heat will rise very sharply.

Raking the fire into a new shape controls its heat rapidly. After a few tries it becomes second nature to rearrange the coals as necessary during cooking periods. Separating briquets lowers heat over the entire fire bed. Concentrating them in a deep layer raises the temperature immediately above them markedly. For kabobs, arrange charcoal in rows, setting kabobs on grill above spaces between briquets.

Cooking distances are frequently changed by the experienced outdoor chef who has learned to disturb his fire as little as possible once it is burning with an even glow and has been arranged to cover an area slightly larger than the food to be grilled. Instead he controls the cooking heat by pulling skillets or packages wrapped in foil toward the hot center or away from it, and by raising and lowering the grill.

All but the simplest braziers are equipped with a revolving grill that also may be moved up and down by a lever. These are an emphatic help since even an inch makes a marked difference in the amount of heat reaching the food. Lacking this equipment, the indispensable two-sided racks can substitute, propped at an angle or raised above a fixed grill on bricks or small stones.

Drip and Flare Control

Flare-ups will cause meat to taste of burned fat; so it is important that they be controlled during grilling.

Cut off most of the outside fat on steaks and chops as the first step. If the meat is marbled with much fat, arrange the coals around a drip pan, or in a circle that leaves the center of the fire bed open so that melting fat drops into a layer of sand or gravel instead of on the coals.

Many outdoor chefs keep a water pistol at hand and use a few drops to knock out unwanted flames. A little of this goes a long way. Food will be steamed instead of broiled and heat will be lowered too much for good results unless water is used sparingly. Water bulbs, such as those used for sprinkling potted plants, or a clothes sprinkler work very well also.

EQUIPMENT

The cost of equipment for outdoor cooking ranges from small units costing as little as $3 to elaborate outfits costing over $300.

If you have not yet had any firsthand experience with open fire cooking, resist that temptation to build a handsome stone or brick barbecue pit that looks so dramatic in the Smiths' backyard, or to invest in that dazzling mobile unit on which the Joneses roast 25 pound turkeys. Only by some happy trials and a few errors can you possibly decide which unit or combination of units will give you and your family the most satisfaction.

Start with a makeshift or really cheap grill. Discover for yourself if cooking anywhere in the patio means filling the whole house with smoke. Find out which eating area is sheltered from blowing heat and sparks. Find out by becoming familiar with the techniques of outdoor cooking how much of it you really want to do and how you really want to use your outdoor dining room—for informal family meals or for entertaining large groups as well.

Your first small grill will not be wasted. After it has served its enormously valuable experimental purpose it will continue to be useful. A collapsible one can be moved easily in the car to picnic grounds. It can also be turned to good account as a supplementary unit for grilling of appetizers, or when the children want to toast marshmallows or hot dogs at their own end of the garden.

Folding grills are the simplest of cooking units next to a grid from the oven propped on stones or bricks. These are rectangular fire boxes supported by folding legs and topped with a grill. They are light, easy to clean, and pack compactly for easy transportation or storage. They are mainly useful for preparation of small, simple meals, though experts can turn out feasts on them.

Bucket and drum grills are light, easily portable, and about the size of large pails. They are especially useful for picnics since fuel can be packed in them all ready to kindle without delay. Some have tops that serve as skillets when reversed.

Hibachis, the small decorative cast-iron firebowls from the Orient, are popular with small boat owners and indoor fireplace cooks. They are excellent for use at picnic sites reached by car, but are too heavy to carry any distance. They come in several sizes. The tiny ones make dramatic centerpieces for tables and are fun for guests who like to grill their own appetizers.

Homemade mobile grills are simple to make if you have a metal wheelbarrow, and serve as a good experimental unit at practically no cost. Line the bottom of the wheelbarrow with heavy aluminum foil. Cover it with 4 inches of clean gravel for a fire bed. Buy a piece of iron mesh big enough to prop across the sides. Get a bag of briquets and you are in business.

Braziers are the most popular units today. There is a wide variety of them. Braziers are round, shallow firebowls set on three long or short legs. If you decide to start with one of these, choose one with an adjustable grill that can be raised or lowered in one of many fashions. All but the cheapest have this feature which is of prime advantage in controlling cooking heat. Many modestly priced braziers have a draft door in the bottom of the firebowl, a great aid in heat control. Others have collars and hoods to shield the fire from wind, wheels for easy changing of location, and stout handles for the same purpose.

EQUIPMENT

Folding Grill

Brazier

Bucket Grill

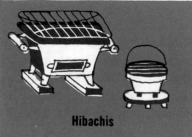

Hibachis

Homemade Mobile Grill

Suitcase Folding Grill

Elaborate Brazier

Cooking Table

Elaborate Cooking Table

Cooking Kettle

Vertical Grill

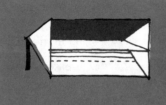

Reflector Oven

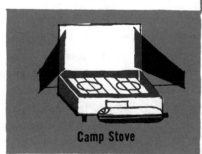

Camp Stove

Stationary Barbecue

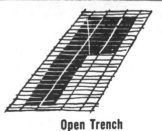

Open Trench

Bean Hole

Cooking tables and wagons, in their simplest form, are braziers with attached working surfaces and shelves. The more elaborate ones rival the glossiest of kitchen ranges in number of gadgets. They have warming ovens, baking ovens, self-lighters, spits, and hooded rotisseries driven by electricity, not to mention cutting boards, storage drawers, towel racks, and rubber tires. They are magnificent, but they still can't cook by themselves. You may want one eventually, but don't invest until you have mastered the art of barbecuing and know whether you want to serve a standing rib roast or bigger and better steaks.

Cooking kettles are something like monster Dutch ovens on legs. They are made of heavy cast iron and have dampers in both bowl and lid. They are sturdy, higher in cost than most braziers, and adaptable to many uses.

Vertical grills are forging ahead fast in popularity though they are not so dramatic in effect as the flat fire glowing under a rack of sizzling food. The great advantage of the vertical grill is its structure which prevents fat from falling into the fire and driving greasy smoke and soot into grilling meat. The fire box or boxes are upright. Grilling racks are suspended in front or between them. Drippings fall into a pan instead of the fire bed, so it is easier to save that good liquid for basting, to control flaring, and to clean up.

Reflector ovens are supplementary equipment for use at the side of any fire. These are boxes of tin or other bright metal with one side open and the others set at angles that catch and bounce heat against the breads, biscuits, or cookies set to bake on the level bottoms. They are usually collapsible since they are used most often on packtrips. There is not much point in using one in the backyard, but they are valuable on a long camping trip since they produce excellent hot breads without taking up room over the fire.

Camp stoves and ovens are wonderfully efficient and compact units that operate on bottled fuel. They are the treasures of vacationers who are covering a lot of ground each day because they can be set up fast and produce a hot meal as quickly as you can get the pots on. No new skills are needed to operate them since their principle is the same as that of gas ranges. They are strictly for pot and pan cooking, however. If you want that heavenly smell and taste of charcoal broiled meats, build a campfire and save the stove for boiling, baking, and heating water for washing up.

Camp ovens are separate units to be used on top of a camp stove. With them you can make hot breads in a jiffy.

Stationary barbecues may be built in any size and material from field stones to hand-painted glazed tiles. Many kitchens in new homes have a permanent open grill built into one wall so that the delights of charcoal broiled food may be enjoyed no matter what the weather may be. The indoor grill as well as the outdoor barbecue pit of brick or stone are matters for the architect and the expert. Once he has some experience with outdoor cooking, a garden barbecue pit is not too difficult for the do-it-yourself mason to construct, and there are many excellent books containing plans drawn to scale and clear step-by-step instructions.

But take a heartfelt word of advice. Spend at least one summer experimenting with a mobile unit before you improve your property with that dramatic stone or brick hearth and chimney. Remember, it is a permanent improvement—or a permanent white elephant if it smokes you or your neighbors out of house or garden.

Open pits and trenches are best adapted for broiling a very large number of split chickens or tender small steaks. Again a word of warning: feeding the whole Sunday School is not a job for the amateur, no matter how good a cook. Try this method on a small scale before you attempt to collect enough helpers—and firewood—to handle a crowd.

Dig a trench 18 inches wide, 18 inches deep, and as long as needed. If using a hardwood fire, have it roaring two hours before you plan to use it and let it burn down to a deep bed of coals. If using briquets, have the coals heaped deeper than usual so that heat will last during the whole cooking period since it will be hard to renew it. Cover the trench with strong chicken wire or fence mesh for a grid. Broil your meats on this, basting and turning frequently. Corn roasted in soaked husks lends itself well to this fire, if you need enough to feed dozens of people.

Fire pits have their important place in outdoor cookery though their demands on time are so stringent that the average chef thinks twice before digging one.

The fire pit is a hole, usually 2 to 4 feet deep and wide enough to accommodate, without crowding, packages of heavily wrapped food. First the hole is lined with dry rocks or bricks. A roaring fire is allowed to burn until the stones are blazing hot and the fire is reduced to glowing coals—2 to 4 hours at the least. A shallow layer of sand or gravel and then seaweed, grass, ferns, or sweet leaves are added to protect the food from charring contact with the coals. The food is well wrapped for the same purpose in fabric, foil, or banana leaves, for example. Sometimes the food is covered with a sheet of corrugated iron topped with some of the hot coals before earth is shoveled on and tamped down. Sometimes a sheet of dampened burlap or canvas is used. After being covered by a foot or more of earth, the food is left to steam for several hours or a whole day, depending on the size of fire and feast. It takes experience to gauge the length of cooking time needed. Better experiment with a small fire pit (not too far from your own stove in case of disappointment) before planning to serve a large hungry crowd.

Bean holes operate on the same principle as fire pits. Dig a hole about twice as deep and wide as your kettle, which should be cast iron with a heavy lid. Line the hole with rocks or bricks. Allow the fire to burn in it hotly for at least two hours. Take out most of the coals. Put in your hot Dutch oven in which beans have been boiling. Reverse the lid, if possible, and heap the coals on top. Cover with at least 8 inches of earth, and leave it all day or overnight.

Can and kettle clambakes are easier ways to serve a small number. Get a shiny, new galvanized iron garbage can with a well-fitting lid. You will need one big enough to hold a layer of seaweed (or well-soaked corn husks if you are not near the ocean) and all the food without crowding. Dig a fire pit, line it with stones, and get a hot fire going. The fire pit should be deep enough to accommodate ⅔ of the can. Put 6 inches of seaweed or husks in the bottom. Add lobsters, chickens, potatoes, corn, and clams. Add a shallow layer of husks or seaweed. Cover the top of the can with canvas. Shovel on sand at least a foot deep and steam for an hour or longer.

A kettle clambake is even faster and easier, though it will not serve so many. For this you need a large cast-iron kettle with a heavy top or a small stout garbage pail. Put 4 inches of water in the bottom. Add 4 inches of corn husks, well packed down. Add food, cover lightly with 3 inches of soaked husks and the tight lid. Set over a hot fire and steam for 1 hour.

Oyster roasts are popular in the South where hot, steaming sacks are laid across a grill. Then a layer of oysters in the shell (preferably those from salt water areas) is placed on top, covered with a second layer of wet sacks, and steamed for about 30 minutes until the shells begin to open. These are opened and the oysters are eaten directly from the half shell with the individual's preference of sauces and toppings.

Electric Equipment

The taste of food cooked over an open fire is so enticingly good that many of us are tempted to produce every last item of a meal over the coals. Variety is one of the best spices, however, and many people find that charcoal broiled meat seems doubly delicious if appetizers, vegetables, and breads are not permeated with the same appetizing flavor.

No meal is perfect if the hostess spends half of the time in the kitchen. The same is true if the outdoor chef is too busy with many courses from a crowded grill to pay attention to guests. Therefore electrical equipment is invaluable for supplementary dishes, for quick and easy meals on porch or patio, for keeping casseroles hot and at hand, and for apartment dwellers whose neighbors take a dim view of open fires on balconies. If you do not have an electric outlet outside, you'll need a long cord to run into the house.

Electric aids are numerous. The coffeepot and blender are useful in keeping hot and cold drinks in quick ready supply. Toasters and waffle makers are just as useful outside as in. The electrically heated warming trays keep casserole dishes hot and tempting and save endless trotting to the kitchen for steaming refills. Grills, saucepans, bean pots, and poppers are also handy.

Electric skillets, round or square, are one of the most adaptable of cookers. They are superb for pancakes, omelettes, eggs, bacon, and the preparing of sausages to be wrapped in dough and baked over coals. They are unmatched for keeping baked beans, macaroni, or other casserole dishes at the right heat for second and third helpings. They are convenient for warming rolls or French fries.

Electric rotisseries are valuable indoors or out. By far the largest number of families cook over coals for small groups rather than for big parties, but the time always comes when it would be fun to feed all comers and nothing less than a whole turkey or a big roast is practical. This is when the electric rotisserie is a life saver. Use the charcoal grill for corn, potatoes, bread heated in foil, and toasted marshmallows—all easier to deliver right on the dot if the reliable rotisserie is taking the guesswork out of the timing of your main dish. One of the best aids a rotisserie can have is a weight compensator. This is a unit that clamps on the turnspit. Metal weights of varying sizes can be screwed to it to equalize the balance of the meat. It is especially useful with meats that may lose much fat during cooking and so need rebalancing—a messy, difficult task when both meat and spit are blazing hot.

Deep fat fryers are one of the best supplements for the charcoal grill. French fried eggplant, zucchini, or potatoes are superb accompaniments for any barbecued meat or fish; so are corn fritters, deep fried onion rings or parsley. And doughnuts, fresh out of the hot fat, are perfection for breakfast, brunch, or supper under summer sun or starry sky.

Thermometers

If all of the gamble were taken out of charcoal cooking, a good deal of the challenge that makes it so fascinating would go also. There still will be room for the use of plenty of that magic sixth sense that makes a good cook even if you use a thermometer—it is the best guarantee against serving dinner at 10 instead of 8 if you are dealing with large meats.

Grill thermometers tell you the temperature of the fire itself and give you a chance to raise or lower the grill to get the high heat needed for steaks, the lower heat you need for a big roast. The models that can be clamped to a turnspit are especially useful since turkeys and other large roasts need a slow steady heat to cook thoroughly without a burned crust around a raw interior. These give you at a glance the heat at spit level.

The hand as thermometer is a method used by campfire cooks since man first roasted meat. Hold your hand, palm down, over the grill near cooking level. If you can keep it there for 3 seconds, the heat is right for poultry—between 300 and 325°. If you must withdraw your hand under 3 seconds, it is hot enough for steak—between 350 and 400°. Use a timer to count seconds. Or murmur slowly the formula of one of my friends, "One-second-one, two-seconds-two, three-seconds-three."

Meat thermometers are even more useful outside than in the kitchen since your fire is so much more variable. Experience and the knife test (slitting and looking) are your best guides for smaller meats, though there is a convenient gadget for those who do not want to lose one drop of the precious juice. It is an aluminum skewer that flashes a red light in its wooden handle when a thick steak is done to the degree you have set on a dial. A thermometer is so inexpensive compared to the cost of meat (and of dismay if you have not guessed right on timing) that no one can afford to ignore this tool. Insert thermometer parallel to spit rod.

Valuable Small Equipment

Two-sided hinged grills are indispensable. They resemble old-fashioned toasting racks with long handles, but they can be adjusted to hold a slice of bread or a school of little shrimp, or expanded to accommodate a thick fish steak. They are enormously useful in dealing with small items such as frankfurters that need frequent turning and are difficult to handle individually on the grill, or delicate or small foods that may break or fall in the fire in turning. They are invaluable in the case of severe flare-ups from dripping fat or basting fluids. The rack can be snatched aside instantly, leaving room for the cook to control flare or let it burn out harmlessly.

Basket grills serve the same purpose as hinged grills. They are deep enough to hold irregularly shaped foods. A corn popper is a basket grill. They are useful for heating foods such as French fries that need tossing and toasting rather than steaming.

Pressure cookers are one of the best of pots to take on a trip if it is important to save as much time as possible in the turning out of hot meals. They work perfectly on a camp stove. Because they are dangerous if the heat is unsteady, *do not use over an open fire.*

Skewers of many different sizes and kinds are on the market. They range from rapierlike weapons with handsome handles to the wooden pins used by butchers. The most practical for day to day use are of steel. Chinese chopsticks make fine disposable skewers if split, sharpened at one end, and soaked well before using. In a pinch you can easily make your own skewers by cutting a heavy wire at a slant at one end and bending the other into a loop for a handle. And, of course, the first skewers were peeled green wands with a sharpened point.

Skewer racks are sometimes useful over a flat fire bed, though foods *en brochette* broil very well placed directly on the grill and turned frequently by hand. Electrically driven ones to be used on the top of a grill are available, but the non-mechanical ones are very effective. These are no more than two pieces of metal bent at right angles so that they stand steady. They are notched at intervals for the support of the skewers. Long or short skewers are fitted into the notches and kabobs can be turned easily without direct contact with the grid. Any store with a barbecue department is apt to have them.

Basting brushes of several sizes are useful to have at hand—small ones for kabobs, hot dogs, hamburgers, or shrimp; bigger ones for steaks and roasts. A good paintbrush with firmly attached bristles that will not pull out is the most practical. A small cotton dish mop makes a good daub for treating large surfaces. The green top of a compact stick of celery is dramatic; so is a bunch of parsley tied firmly to a long stick. Many people like to use bunches of fresh thyme, sage, marjoram, or other herbs tied to a stick for a basting tool with a built-in seasoning of its own.

Aluminum foil is considered by many experienced barbecue cooks second in importance as a tool only to a good sharp knife, because it can be adapted to so many uses. Line a brazier bowl with it for extra reflected heat and for quick, neat handling of greasy ashes. Use it for quickly fashioned drip pans exactly the shape needed. Prop a band at the edge of a fire for a wind break. Make your own warming oven of it. Heat leaky vegetables, such as frozen peas or beans, in a quickly shaped bowl. Wrap freshly caught fish in it for transportation home if the catch is bigger than needed for a fish fry, and protect the car from that well-known lingering odor. Make cups to hold a basting sauce or fat poured off bacon.

A spectacular wheeled cart can be made by lining a wheelbarrow with foil. Allow edges, cut in points or scallops, to fall over the sides so that the barrow looks like a gigantic silver bowl on wheels. Fill it with cracked ice and embed glasses of iced tea or fruit punch, watermelon slices, or cantaloupe halves in it.

Foil comes in both heavy and light weights, and in narrow as well as standard widths. Heavy-duty foil is needed for food cooked directly on the coals, while the lighter weight may be used for basting cups where heat is less.

For wrapping food, use 12″ wide heavy-duty aluminum foil. Place food on foil a bit off center. Bring foil up over food so edges meet. Fold all open edges toward food, two or more times in at least ½″ folds, sealing securely. To open food, tear or cut off folded ends or snip top and pull open to make its own container.

TIPS FROM EXPERTS

Before any outdoor meal, whether picnic, camping trip, or supper on the terrace, make a list of everything you need. Assemble everything before you start packing or cooking. A picnic is a sad parched affair if drinking water is forgotten. A cookout is no fun if someone has to backtrack miles to store or home for salt and pepper. Keep your outdoor party outdoors.

Set up some kind of a roomy working surface for the chef near the fire—a place for easy reaching of tongs, gloves, seasonings, can opener, water pistol, basting bowl and brush, cutting board, and serving plates. Folding aluminum tables are practical for the outdoors, easy to store, and inexpensive.

Plan the eating area in advance. Have heavy chairs dragged into place near surfaces that can hold glasses and ashtrays. No guest has yet been able to invent a way to hold beverage, cigarette, ashtray, knife, fork, plate, and napkin at the same time. Informality should not mean discomfort.

Have a plan for scraping and stacking of used dishes so that your outdoor living room does not look like a school cafeteria after a stormy lunch period.

Don't try the exotic new recipe for the first time on a big party. Make a trial run for the family first and take the guesswork out of timing and seasoning.

Don't crowd your grill. It is much better to bring out a big casserole of corn pudding at the last minute from the kitchen than to roast fresh ears over the coals while your lucious steak grows cold.

Design your cookout for a change of pace and taste. One or two dishes flavored with smoke seem extra delicious if every other item does not share the same seasoning. Use skillets and foil, ovens and casseroles for some few of your foods.

Expect the unexpected and be flexible. Have an alternate plan worked out in case a sudden summer storm blows up to drench fire and guests. Know where you can move your mobile brazier in an emergency. In the yard a huge sun umbrella will protect the fire in a stationary barbecue pit—and the cook—while guests seek shelter on the porch.

Have something for everyone with the first grilling. It is far better to have one big thick steak than eight small thin ones from a grill that can hold only four at a time.

Have plenty of everything—fire and food alike. The outdoors sharpens appetites. Leftovers are little trouble to bring home and can always be used another day—but nothing can save a meal that is too little and too late.

Don't forget materials for coping with mosquitoes, ants, flies, sunburn, and poison ivy.

And don't forget the salt and pepper!

Terrace Barbecue (see page 47)

Submarines As You Like Them (see page 73)

utdoor Dinner Party (see page 47)

Tailgate Buffet (see page 64)

TOOLS FOR THE OUTDOOR COOK

Half the fun of cooking outdoors disappears if the chef or his aides are forever running to the kitchen, or must waste time rigging makeshifts for the tools designed to make open fire cooking easier. The most successful barbecuers assemble everything needed in advance—napkins, plates, glasses, food, seasonings, tools, and plenty of fuel—and then forget that they have a kitchen for the next happy hours.

Here are the basic utensils you will need for efficient handling of fire and food:

Cotton work gloves for handling briquets

Grilling mitts for hot skewers and pots and for testing and turning foil-wrapped packages

Basting brush

Paring knife

Carving knife and fork

Big serving spoons

Big cutting board for carving

Water bulb, pistol, or sprinkler

A pail of clean water

Hinged grills

Skewers

Pepper grinder and salt shaker

Carry-all box of herbs, spices, and other seasonings

Paper towels

Damp towel for cook's hands

Foil

Spatula

Pancake turner

Two long-handled tongs, one for coals, one for food

Heavy long-handled forks

Pliers for adjusting turnspit holding forks

Garbage pail

A table or some other work surface near the fire

OUTDOOR FEASTS...
AT HOME AND AWAY

BACKYARD OR TERRACE BARBECUES

The word barbecue comes from the French *barbe à queue* which was used at one time to mean a pig or lamb cooked whole "from whiskers to tail." Today the word has a much wider meaning. We use it to describe any meal involving foods, big or little, cooked in the open, whether hot dogs on a hibachi or a turkey on an electric rotisserie.

The barbecue at home is the aristocrat of outdoor meals. Though its mood is informal, food often is as sophisticated and service is as elegant as in a dining room—but much less trouble if plans are carefully made.

This is where women, experienced in the day-to-day organizing of menus and meals, shine. They know the importance of the complete shopping list; of cleaning, or peeling, or otherwise preparing vegetables in advance; of having tools sharp and handy; and of not asking one burner or one oven to produce a whole meal at the same time. There is plenty for everyone to do before and during a big cookout. Most women I know are quite content to concentrate on advance preparations and the duties of a hostess, and leave the more dazzling duties over that hot bed of coals to the males.

If you have a big barbecue unit, or enough supplementary ones, the entire meal can be produced outdoors. It takes an experienced *al fresco* chef to accomplish this, however. Things become a good bit easier if you concentrate on two or three foods cooked on grill or spit and supplement them with casseroles and desserts kept at the proper degree of heat or cold in warming oven or refrigerator until needed.

Though host and hostess naturally do most of the work of cooking and serving, the best parties leave a little something for guests to do. One good idea is to invite them to grill their own appetizers—but not over the main fire! Every outdoor chef needs all of the elbow room he can get. Resist this plan firmly unless you have an extra grill or small table units, such as hibachis, for the use of guests.

A buffet table set up at a reasonable distance from the cooking area is the best way to tempt a large number of guests to join comfortably in the serving. On it can go all of the eating tools, glasses, pitchers of iced tea or fruit punch, the salads set in double bowls of cracked ice, the roast potatoes kept steaming hot in foil wrappings, the condiments and sauces, pickles and chutneys, the hot casseroles on their warming trays or chafing dishes. Each guest takes his plate to the grill, gets his sizzling serving of the main course and perhaps an ear of corn husked by the chef just before serving, a toasted bun or slice of crisp, hot bread, and then moves on to serve himself to the rest of the feast.

Such a buffet is easily set up. Three card tables or metal folding tables covered with a cloth or gaily printed plastic will do it. If you are using card tables on a lawn, set the adjacent legs in tall tin cans. This keeps the tables from spreading apart, holds them steadier for a carver, and prevents the legs from sinking unevenly into the soft grass.

Nearly everyone uses heavy paper napkins for an outdoor meal, and the handsome stout paper plates available in so many patio shops are increasingly popular. Paper cups have their enormously useful place, but I think that they are more suitable to the more casual picnic than to dinner on the terrace. At home, in your own flower-ringed patio or garden, china or pottery plates and cups are far more pleasant —unless, of course, you are serving a very large crowd without extra help.

It is fun to have cookout forks and knives and spoons with wooden or bone handles, but it is also entirely proper to use the same silver for your garden party as you do in your dining room.

Long drinks are better than short ones. Serve fruit or vegetable drinks in tall glasses clinking with ice so that guests will have plenty to sip slowly without bothering the host for refills as he brings his meal to its perfect sizzling peak.

Here are some of the menus for backyard barbecues that we have found especially tempting in combinations of foods and in practicality of cooking and serving.

Recipes for starred items are in the following section.

Steak Barbecue

Chilled Tomato and Chicken Bouillon
*Charcoal Broiled Steak with Bleu Cheese Topping
*Roasted Potatoes and Onions
*Caesar Salad
Corn Bread Toasted on the Grill
*Blueberry Peach Pie
Iced Tea   Coffee

Burger 'N Bean Barbecue

*Double Decker Hamburgers on Toasted Buns
*Summertime Tomato Relish
Baked Beans
*Fruit Kabobs
Brownies
Iced Tea   Milk   Coffee

Beef Kabob Barbecue

Clam Bouillon on the Rocks
*Beef on a Skewer
*Outdoor Indian Pilaf
Split Belgian Endive Salad
French Dressing
Hot Rolls
Cantaloupe filled with Seedless Green Grapes
Iced Tea   Coffee

Veal Steaks Barbecue

Pineapple Juice
*Grilled Veal Steaks
*Outdoor Creamy Cabbage
*Onions Roasted in Foil
Romaine Salad
Herbed French Dressing
*Hot Poppy Seed French Loaf
Ice Cream
Crushed Strawberry Sauce
Iced Tea   Coffee

Chicken Barbecue

Frosty Orange Nog
(orange juice with whole egg beaten in)
*Chicken Teriyaki Barbecue
*Roasted Sweet Potatoes
Iceberg Lettuce Wedges
Sour Cream and Caper Dressing
*Hot Herbed French Loaf
*Aloha Chiffon Cake
Iced Tea   Coffee

Terrace Barbecue

(Pictured on pages 34-35.)

*Whole Barbecued Turkey
*Stuffed Acorn Squash
*Tossed Salad with Cauliflowerets
Poppy Seed Rolls
*Chocolate Butter-Mallow Cake
Milk   Coffee

At the Poolside

(Pictured on pages 140-141.)

*Beef Roast on the Turnspit
*Potatoes Roasted in Foil
with various toppings
(melted butter, sour cream, bacon bits)
*Peas Almondine in Foil
*Tomatoes Vinaigrette
Pumpernickel Bread
*French Glacé Fruit Tarts
Iced Tea   Coffee
Baked Beans

Outdoor Dinner Party

(Pictured on pages 38-39.)

*Marge's Lamb Shish-Kabobs
Au Gratin Potatoes
Relish Tray
Bread Sticks
*Upside-down Apple Pecan Pie
Iced Tea   Coffee

SHORE COOKING

A meal cooked at the lake or seashore is quite a different challenge to the outdoor chef from the backyard barbecue since no kitchen facilities or supplies are at hand. It also is quite different from packtrip cooking which must depend on food easily transported in greater quantity and kept fresh for perhaps several days.

The menus featured on pp. 50-51 are for a one-meal outing with all items carried, usually by car, to a fairly distant site. Therefore, the first rule is to make a list of everything you may need and check off each item as it is packed. A corn roast is a disaster if grilling mitts and butter are forgotten. And don't forget plenty of water for drinking and washing of hands, hard-water soap, and paper towels.

The most successful shore meals are those that are kept simple. Concentrate on one excellent main dish. Have plenty of it (and then some!) because sun, wind, and swimming bring everyone to the feast with ravenous appetites.

Choose pre-assembled side dishes that need not be served either very hot or very cold. Make desserts that may be transported in their own baking pans, such as pies, chocolate squares, cheesecake, or iced loaf cake.

Ideally, shore cooking is done on a wood fire. However, just in case there isn't a splinter of driftwood for miles along your favorite beach, toss a sack of briquets into the car.

The experienced shore cook carries a hatchet, of course, and a canvas windbreak to protect the fire from strong breezes which may send smoke and sparks streaming, or may dust a succulent steak with gritty flying sand.

A stone boat is valuable. This is a stout strip of canvas about a yard long with loops or handles at each end. Driftwood or cut logs or stones may be piled on it, and a far greater load than one person can lift or carry may be dragged easily.

You'll find a shovel useful, and you will need a flat grill or grid that may be supported by logs or rocks above the fire.

Shore breezes always seem deceptively cool, but remember that the sun is hot. Food or drink in glass or tin or foil becomes unappetizingly warm very quickly if left unprotected in the direct rays.

If you are bringing salad from home, choose one that can be assembled in advance, such as potato, mixed vegetable, or cole slaw. Cover top of bowl with waxed paper. Chill it in its container thoroughly. Then wrap it in half a dozen layers of wet newspaper. Do the same for bottled drinks even if you are carrying an insulated pail of ice to chill them. Lacking such equipment or the time to pre-chill drinks, submerge bottles as soon as you arrive in a shady part of lake or stream, or bury them in the cold sand at the edge of the surf. And mark the spot! An incoming tide can level sand in moments, or drown your bottles under many feet of crashing waves.

No outdoor feast is over until you have left the site as clean as you found it—or cleaner! This job will not be a chore if you follow the simple suggestions given below.

Toss cartons, paper cups, plates, napkins, and wrappings into the fire. See that they are burned to grey ash, not just half-charred litter to be spread by the wind.

Take empty bottles and cans home, or bury them deep and well above the water line where winter tides cannot find and reduce them to dangerous splinters.

Drench your fire, stir it, and then drench again, making sure that no single smoldering spark remains. All it takes is one breeze-flung ember to reduce a tree-sheltered shore to a cinder patch that will be an eyesore for years to come.

Fish Fry at the Shore

Whether you start early and hope to catch your own, or buy your fish from a commercial angler, a fish fry is one of the most pleasant of shore meals and one of the easier ways to feed a sizable crowd.

Small whole fish such as trout or smelt are most often used. Larger fish such as muskellunge or the smaller walleyed pike, bass, halibut, and catfish are equally suitable if filleted or cut into small steaks. All are delicious fried to a golden brown, crisp outside, tender and steaming within.

Take plenty of skillets. Fried fish must not be crowded in the pan. Take along plenty of whatever cooking fat you choose. You haven't brought enough unless you have a little left over!

Mix dry ingredients at home for the justly famous Hush Puppies that are the classic bread for this event. Then all you need is water when ready to drop the batter into sizzling fat.

In addition to the usual gear, you'll need a knife for scaling fish.

*Fried Fish
Cole Slaw
*Hush Puppies
Watermelon or Fresh Fruit in Season
*New Fudge Cake
Coffee

Corn Roast at the Shore

Buy tender young ears direct from the field if you can. Remove the silk but not the husks. Dump them in an anchored burlap sack to soak for an hour in a clear stream or the sea. Salt water makes them twice as good.

*Roast Corn
Butter and Salt
Cold Sliced Tongue, Ham, or Meat Loaf
Rye Bread and Butter Sandwiches
Dill Pickles   Mustard   Sweet Pickles
*Jack Horner Cake
Coffee

Wiener Roast on the Sand Dunes

(*Pictured on page 137.*)

Wieners Toasted on Sticks
*Speedy Baked Beans
Potato Chips
Watermelon Wedges
*Angels' Halos
Soft Drinks

"Down-East" Clambake

(*Pictures and directions on pages 52-53.*)

*Steamed Lobsters   *Steamed Clams
Drawn Butter
Hot Corn on the Cob
Sweet Potatoes   Onions
Relishes   Rolls
Watermelon

"Down-East" Clambake . .

1. William G. Foster of York Harbor, Me. has devised a new clambake method using a steel plate. A roaring fire is built under the plate, which rests on steel side panels.

2. It is then covered with about 6″ of wet rockweed, cut from the rocks at low tide. A wooden box with a wire mesh bottom (½″ galvanized hardware cloth) is placed on top.

3. Next the food is put in the box according to cooking time: lobsters on the bottom layer; unhusked fresh corn (silk removed), sweet potatoes, and onions in the middle.

4. Clams, soaked overnight and rinsed of sand, go on top. Water is poured over the food to ensure plenty of steam. The clam juice then steams through, flavoring all the foods.

A Brand New Technique

5. As quickly as possible, the box of food is covered with a large sheet of heavy, clean cotton duck canvas or flame-proof cloth. Care must be taken not to burn the canvas.

6. All the loose ends of the covering are carefully tucked in around the box. This is an important step, holding the heat in the box while keeping the wind off the bake.

7. For extra protection, the canvas is covered with more wet rockweed. The heat rising through the first layer of rockweed gives a distinctive flavor to the food.

8. After an hour or so has passed, the lobsters should be done. Brush off the rockweed, lift up the canvas, and get ready to dig in to a fine feast. (See pages 142-143.)

SEASIDE IN THE BACKYARD

There is no need to live near the shore to enjoy the delights of barbecued fish and shellfish. Magnificent deep sea, lake, and mountain stream fish are now available, iced or frozen, in every one of our states. Many people automatically think of meats when they think of barbecuing. In my opinion, fish, almost more than any other food, becomes immeasurably more tempting when grilled over charcoal, if properly basted and handled.

Kettle or Can Clambake

(See page 23 for directions.)

Kettle Baked Lobsters and Clams
Melted Salted Butter   Lemon Wedges
*Roast Corn
*French Bread
Watermelon
*Coconut Lemon Bars
Coffee

Fish Steaks Barbecue

*Swordfish Steaks
Lemon Wedges
*Grilled Carrot Sticks
Avocado, Lettuce, and Tomato Salad
French Dressing
Toasted Corn Bread Squares
Fruit Compote
*Almond Dips
Iced Tea   Coffee

Whole Fish Barbecue

A whole fish glistening under its basting sauce is one of the most dramatic sights the outdoor chef can provide. And it tastes as good as it looks.

*Whole Barbecued Salmon
*Garden Stuffing
Lemon Wedges
Scalloped Potato Casserole
*Green Beans with Mushrooms and Onions
Hot Chive Bread
*Vagabond Strawberry Shortcake
Iced Tea   Coffee

Shellfish Barbecue

The Scallop Kabobs or Shrimp Carmel are easy to assemble and fast cooking—a good choice for a cook-out serving both early and late comers.

*Scallop Kabobs or *Shrimp Carmel
*Potatoes Roasted in the Coals
Tomato and Lettuce Salad
French Dressing
Hot Hard Rolls
*Peach Caramel Shortcake
Iced Tea   Coffee

Lobster Feast

This is an impressive feast and you do not need to be within driving distance of the ocean to enjoy it. Live Maine lobsters can be ordered from several companies that make a specialty of shipping choice ones by fast freight. They are packed in seaweed, then in a cooking container, then in ice and a shipping container. They are often ordered for parties 1,800 miles from their New England waters.

If you want steamed lobsters, all you do is put the cooking container on the fire and follow instructions that come with it for cooking time. Some orders include fresh clams in the shell and a canned Indian Pudding so dear to the palates of "Down-Easters."

If you want to broil your lobsters, you will find instructions in the next section.

*Grilled Lobster
Melted Butter   Lemon Wedges
*Roasted Potatoes and Onions
*Peanut Crunch Slaw
*Garlic Bread
Grilled Peaches 'N Berries
Iced Tea   Coffee

1. Tear off claws. Crack with nutcracker or lobster shears.

2. Arch back until tail breaks off. Break flippers off tailpiece.

3. Insert fork into tailpiece where flippers broke and push.

4. Unhinge body from back for meat. Claws have meat, too.

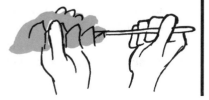

COOKING AFLOAT

Cooking afloat is another kind of special challenge and opportunity whether you have a real galley or one small unit that operates on canned heat. Even a small craft with any kind of a cabin usually has sizable lockers. Basic foods for a week or more of cruising can be stored in an astonishingly small space if you stock and stow away wisely.

Dry supplies such as sugar are best transferred from paper or cardboard packages to tins with tight lids to keep out the damp. Jars are less practical unless stored in some fashion that prevents rolling around and shattering. One of my sea-going friends uses empty soft drink carriers for this purpose, but plastic or metal containers are by far the safest. For a one-day cruise, insulated portable lockers are useful for carrying ice, salads, and bottled soft drinks, and for carrying back extra fish if you are lucky.

The concentrated foods described under Packtrips (p. 65) are just as useful for the cruising camper as for the deep woodsman.

Restricted cooking and eating space should not mean a meager diet. One of the most impressive outdoor meals I ever had was served on a small sailing boat without a galley.

We anchored in a protected cove after an afternoon of brisk running before the wind. While the "captain" dropped sail, his wife lighted a small heating unit that was fixed to the cabin wall and slung on gimbals so that the pot itself could ride steady while the boat rocked. In this she heated a can of asparagus tips, and later, water for coffee. While she was setting up a table that slipped firmly into slots, the captain threw a double handful of charcoal sticks into a hibachi. The breeze made it catch and burn to smokeless coals quickly. While a steak was grilling, the rest of the meal was assembled—sliced tomatoes, homemade bread, a mélange of canned fruits, and a tinned white fruitcake. As the sunset flared and lights began to twinkle on shore we ate a meal that anyone would have served without apology in a dining room— and then sailed home under the starry sky.

Some seasoned cooks afloat prefer the one dish meal and dessert that just require reheating. While the delicious, sizzling main course is being eaten, a fruit pie or crisp is heating for dessert. Salad and coffee from a thermos are the only additions you need for a meal like this.

Here are suggestions for meals easy to assemble on a boat.

Fish Stew Dinner

A fish stew, one of the best of one dish meals, is easy to make aboard ship when serving a crowd. There are almost as many variants as there are mariners. Bouillabaisse is the famous specialty of French seacoasts. It features lobsters, shrimp, mussels, and chunks of firm-fleshed fish in a rich soup flavored with tomato, saffron, and lots of garlic. Chowders are the New England way with fish stew, and gloriously satisfying they are with crusty bread or crisp crackers. On the West Coast, chippino is popular. It is a mélange of any fish or shellfish handy, plenty of fresh vegetables, and garlic.

*Bouillabaisse
French Bread and Butter
Canned Pears
Maraschino Sauce
*Chocolate Chip Bars
Coffee

One Burner Stove Dinner

*Tagliarini
Vienna Bread
Pickled Beets
Sliced Onions and Cucumbers
*Date Nut Chews
Bananas, Tangerines, Apples
Coffee

Hibachi Dinner I

*Grilled Lamb Chops
Canned Whole New Potatoes
(tossed in butter and caraway seeds)
Carrot and Zucchini Sticks
Herb Dressing
*Blushing Apple Upside-down Cake
Coffee

Hibachi Dinner II

*Sea Food Jambalaya
Mixed Green Salad with French Dressing
*Strawberry-Rhubarb Puff
Coffee (from thermos)

CRUISING ON LAND

Each year by the hundreds of thousands more families are taking to the open road when vacation time comes. Some content themselves with no more than a small immersion unit which makes a practically instantaneous cup of hot coffee or tea in a motel, and vacuum bottles for cold milk and juices.

An increasing number of families are learning the pleasures and economy of being independent of the sometimes second-rate food served at roadside snack bars or the wearying wait for service in crowded, noisy restaurants, and are carrying a carton of staples and a portable camp stove in the back of the car.

Each year many more holiday wanderers are investing in sleeping-out as well as cooking-out equipment and return singing the praises of the special freedoms of station wagon and trailer camping.

Equipment can be as simple or as elaborate and dramatic as you choose. One valuable and comparatively inexpensive item is a canvas paravane or roof that attaches to the top of the car and shelters your table and portable stove from the sun or the shower that might just blow up and drench your feast at the moment of serving. These come in gay colors, plain or striped. Some have sides which may be dropped to form a cabaña for changing swimsuits or for shelter from wind.

Don't underestimate the comfort and convenience of folding tables and chairs. Tables now come in wonderfully compact units that roll into small cylinders when not in use and can be tucked away anywhere in the car. Sitting on the ground for a picnic is fun, but it loses its charm quickly if repeated three times a day.

No matter how luxuriously or how modestly you choose to cruise on land, appetizing hot meals that can be turned out with the minimum of time and effort should be your main concern. Everyone is comfortably tired after a day of driving and sight-seeing. It is no pleasure for a hungry family, and no holiday for mother, if dinner takes all evening to prepare.

This does not mean that you have to resign yourself to a diet of canned foods. One of the great advantages of traveling by car is that somewhere along every road wonderful fresh fruits, vegetables, and meats may be picked up. All you need are a few cans of emergency rations and the usual staples such as sugar, flour, and seasonings, plus one of the many models of the efficient camp stoves and ovens that operate on bottled fuel.

A special delight I take in new places is the sampling of foods for which the region is noted. Let your holiday be a change in every way. Canned beans are delicious—but they can be had any day of the year at home. When rolling through Massachusetts, try picking up a piping-hot pot of the sweet and salty beans made in the New England manner—a sensational novelty to westerners. Buy boiled lobsters hot out of a lobster pound in Maine, and serve them with that state's famous potatoes and fresh corn roasted over your own campfire. Try building a meal around the delicately smoked Ciscoes sold along the shores of Lake Superior north of Duluth; or around the buttery fresh-smoked shrimp offered at stands along the east coast of Florida; or around fresh tamales in the southwest; fresh tuna and langouste in California.

All over the country, be sure to explore "Cake Sale" signs outside of churches. I never miss one if I can help it. The best cooks of the congregation vie with each other to produce the prettiest and best cakes for such benefits. So you have the double reward of aiding a good cause and finding a superb homemade dessert without trouble.

Following are suggestions for solid, well-balanced meals that can be turned out in less than an hour once a family has established a routine for sensible shopping along the way, sharing the unpacking, and setting up the equipment for cooking and eating.

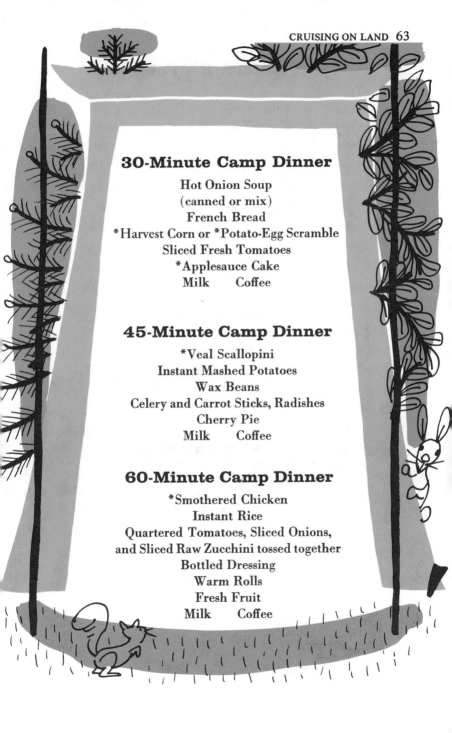

30-Minute Camp Dinner

Hot Onion Soup
(canned or mix)
French Bread
*Harvest Corn or *Potato-Egg Scramble
Sliced Fresh Tomatoes
*Applesauce Cake
Milk   Coffee

45-Minute Camp Dinner

*Veal Scallopini
Instant Mashed Potatoes
Wax Beans
Celery and Carrot Sticks, Radishes
Cherry Pie
Milk   Coffee

60-Minute Camp Dinner

*Smothered Chicken
Instant Rice
Quartered Tomatoes, Sliced Onions,
and Sliced Raw Zucchini tossed together
Bottled Dressing
Warm Rolls
Fresh Fruit
Milk   Coffee

Dinner in a Pot

This is practical if most of the family wants a swim or hike before the evening meal, and there is time to simmer a stew before their return—otherwise, carry a pressure cooker!

*Lamb Stew
with Carrots, Diced Potatoes, Fresh Peas
Parsley Dumplings
Radishes   Pickles
Fresh or Canned Fruit
Cookies
Milk   Coffee

Hot Weather Supper

At the end of a blazing hot day all you may feel like preparing or eating is something cool and quick but filling. Here is a good combination easily bought along the road.

Avocado or Lettuce Cups
stuffed with canned crabmeat mixed with mayonnaise
Canned Asparagus Tips
Sliced Tomatoes
Whole Wheat Bread
Cheesecake
Milk   Iced Coffee

Tailgate Buffet
(*Pictured on page 40.*)

*Meat Balls with Puff Biscuits
Carrot and Celery Sticks, Cherry Tomatoes,
Radish Roses, and Stuffed Green Olives
*Camp Oven Gingerbread

PACKTRIP COOKING

Trips by horseback or canoe into wilderness and roadless areas are immeasurably more easy for the camp cook today than in the past because of the very large variety of condensed and dehydrated foods available.

Any supermarket offers dried soups in envelopes, dried milk, ready-mix pastries and puddings, and fruit concentrate powders. Butter, bacon, cheese, and meats come in cans. Buy these in small sizes so that the supply for the whole trip does not have to be tossed out after the first few days in the hot summer sun.

Few people who are planning a first packtrip—or motor trip for that matter—realize what an impressively large list of dehydrated delicacies as well as basic foods are offered by professional outfitters. I did not until one summer when I was driving with friends through northern Minnesota. We needed flashlight batteries, and stopped for them in Ely which is on the edge of the vast roadless area embraced by our Superior National Forest and Canada's huge and equally magnificent Quetico National Forest.

By lucky chance, we happened to choose an outfitter's shop instead of a hardware store. Instead of five minutes for our purchase, we spent the rest of the afternoon marveling at the stock, buying many samples to test, and listening to anecdotes about the varied demands outfitters can satisfy. For example, one impetuous client and his wife arrived in formal dinner clothes by chartered plane early one morning—and before lunch were paddling north, completely outfitted: canoe, hatchet, can opener, cooking and fishing gear, sleeping bags, all rented. They had bought bright mackinaws and all other needed clothing as well as a week's supply of food including such luxuries for the wilderness as a plastic envelope of dried, concentrated maple syrup. It is expensive to get all new clothing at the last minute for roughing it in the wilderness, but less expensive to rent camp gear unless you are sure of giving your own steady use.

Outfitters know the basic secret of comfortable packtripping which is "Take all you need, but no more." One skillet is often better than two, especially if you have learned the secret of saving pans by making skewer or bayonet breads. You will find recipes for them in the recipe section.

If you are planning to live partially on the land, supplementing basic foods with what fish, fowl, or game you can forage, take some trial runs at home with the techniques used by campers for baking birds and fish in a shield of clay.

A packtrip can be a glorious holiday or a miserable, if not actually dangerous, experience. I strongly advise making your first such trip with a professional guide or other knowledgeable camper who knows all of the tricks of cooking in rain and wind, and of stowing supplies so that you do not find yourself with everything, including matches, at the bottom of a lake two long hard days from replacements.

Packtrip Breakfast

(*Pictured on page 144.*)

*Grilled Canadian Bacon and Sausages
*Pancakes and Syrup
Hot Coffee

Packtrip Lunch

Chicken-Noodle Soup
Canned Baked Beans
Canned Brown Bread
Milk and Chocolate Milk
(made from non-fat dry milk)

Packtrip Fisherman's Dinner

*Pan Fried Fresh Fish
Peas and Corn
(heated in opened can)
*Bayonet Bread
Canned Fruit
*Welsh Cakes
Coffee

Packtrip Hunter's Dinner

(Hunters do not dine on what they shoot, but bring their trophies home.)

Beef Stew or Chili Con Carne
*Onion Butter Biscuits
Individual Relish Packets
Fruit Turnovers
Coffee

BREAKFAST COOKOUTS

This is a favorite festivity all through cowboy country, and a popular feature of dude ranch holidays. Guests take off in the early morning, ride for an hour to where a cook wagon is waiting in some pretty glade or hilltop, and a fire is sending out tempting aromas and welcome sizzling sounds.

Professionals usually prepare these feasts, but some of my friends find the idea so good that they feature much the same food for brunch cookouts in their own yards or at the shore.

You'll need a big coffeepot, a couple of big skillets, double grills, for toasting bread or muffins—and plenty of food!

It is a good idea to measure into a jar or plastic container the amount of pancake mix or biscuit mix that you will need, leaving out only the liquid. Carry the mix in a roomy container so that the batter can be stirred in its carrying can or jar. Break eggs and carry them much more easily and safely in a screw-top container.

Keep the coffee going.

And don't forget the salt and pepper!

Midwest Special

Orange Juice
*Blueberry Pancakes with Syrup
*Grilled Pork Chops
Scrambled Eggs
Toasted English Muffins
Coffee

All on a Griddle

Tomato Juice
Fried Sausage
Eggs Sunny-Side-Up
Fried Potatoes
*Hot Butter Cakes
Jelly   Butter   Honey
Coffee

Frankly Fancy

Apple Juice
Wild Rice Pancakes
Hot Smoked Kippers
Bacon
Scrambled Eggs in Cream
Toast
Maple Syrup
Coffee

Midsummer Delight

Melon Wedges
*Hearty Ham Steak
Hominy Grits
*Superb Coffee Cake
Coffee

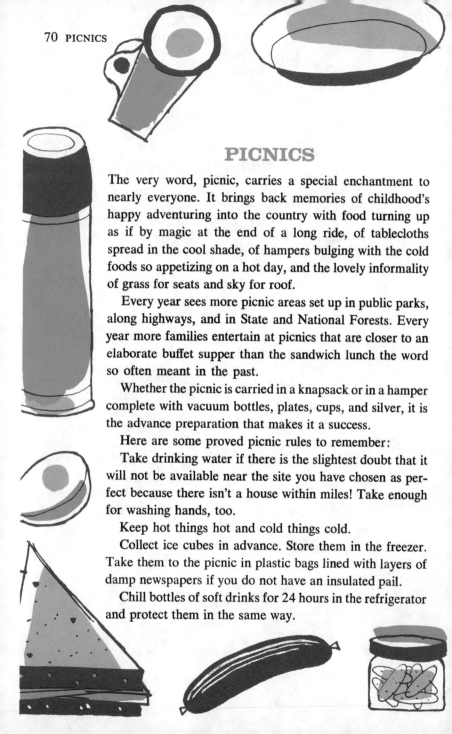

PICNICS

The very word, picnic, carries a special enchantment to nearly everyone. It brings back memories of childhood's happy adventuring into the country with food turning up as if by magic at the end of a long ride, of tablecloths spread in the cool shade, of hampers bulging with the cold foods so appetizing on a hot day, and the lovely informality of grass for seats and sky for roof.

Every year sees more picnic areas set up in public parks, along highways, and in State and National Forests. Every year more families entertain at picnics that are closer to an elaborate buffet supper than the sandwich lunch the word so often meant in the past.

Whether the picnic is carried in a knapsack or in a hamper complete with vacuum bottles, plates, cups, and silver, it is the advance preparation that makes it a success.

Here are some proved picnic rules to remember:

Take drinking water if there is the slightest doubt that it will not be available near the site you have chosen as perfect because there isn't a house within miles! Take enough for washing hands, too.

Keep hot things hot and cold things cold.

Collect ice cubes in advance. Store them in the freezer. Take them to the picnic in plastic bags lined with layers of damp newspapers if you do not have an insulated pail.

Chill bottles of soft drinks for 24 hours in the refrigerator and protect them in the same way.

Chill salads in heavy pottery casseroles for easy serving and appetizing coldness.

A steaming pot of chili beans will hold heat for several hours if wrapped first in foil and then in newspapers.

Make chicken or potato salad and chill thoroughly; take to picnic in refrigerator containers. Omit raw vegetables from this process, but carry washed lettuce, radishes, and green onions in a plastic bag, sliced tomatoes in jars. Sliced cucumbers and carrot sticks are doubly good if popped right in with the French dressing and allowed to marinate on the way.

Individual portions of cottage cheese, cold baked beans, and salads of chicken, tuna, macaroni, or potato are conveniently served if packed in waxed paper cups.

Cakes are best transported in their baking pans.

Pies travel well between paper plates taped together.

Much last minute flurry can be saved by making sandwiches of meat, cheese, or any non-leaky filling the night before and storing in the refrigerator. Use butter rather than mayonnaise which soaks into bread and makes it soggy if too long in contact.

In hot weather avoid cream puffs or anything else containing a mixture of milk or cream with eggs unless you have a portable refrigerator. A few hours is enough, under certain circumstances, to make these dangerous. There are so many dozens of other tempting desserts, don't take a chance and risk food poisoning.

And don't forget the salt and pepper.

Brown Paper Bag Picnic

This is a specialty of one of my friends, and a good idea it is for any large family, or picnic party. First on the list is stout paper bags that will not tear easily. Into each goes paper plate, cup, napkins, disposable wooden spoons, and a carefully wrapped lunch. All of the individual lunch bags are stored in a roomy carton in the back of the car with an insulated pail of ice for drinking water, a vacuum jug of hot coffee, another for cold milk. A small knapsack holds the extras such as salt and pepper shakers, mustard, a bar of soap, paper towels, a bug bomb, and suntan lotion.

Once the cars are parked, each member of the party takes charge of his own lunch while several of the huskier ones tote the jugs and bottles. In this way, the load is not too heavy for any one person. The party is free to ramble and climb until the ideal view is discovered, and there is no delay while food in big portions is unwrapped and served.

*Stuffed Eggs
*Choice of Sandwiches
Cold Baked Beans in Paper Cups
Pickles   Radishes
Pear, Peach, Apple, or Tangerine
Cookies
Lemonade (made with powdered concentrate)
Milk   Coffee

Hamper Picnic

Traditionally, picnics mean cold foods, but that is no reason they cannot be as sophisticated as you choose. Indeed, many of the most elaborate lunches I have had came out of the big fitted hampers that are so popular and that make picnicking so graceful and easy.

Cold Grape Juice
Smoked Rainbow Trout Pâté
or Smoked Fish on Small Crackers
Cold Fried Chicken
Cooked and Raw Vegetable Salad
Caper Mayonnaise
Whole Cherry Tomatoes   Watermelon Pickles
*Herb Bread and Butter Sandwiches
*Leaf O' Gold Cake
Chocolate Peppermints
Coffee

Picnic by a Stream

(*Pictured on page 33.*)

*Southern Fried Chicken
*Potato Salad
Assorted Sandwiches
(Have a different color sandwich wrapping for each filling.
See page 154 for sandwich suggestions.)
Frosted Cupcakes
Iced Tea

Submarines As You Like Them

(*Pictured on pages 36-37.*)

*Submarines
Relishes on Ice
*Watermelon Supreme
Assorted Cold Drinks

RECIPES FOR OUTDOOR DINING

The delights of dining *al fresco* are as numerous as the family groups who enjoy this pastime across the country.

A few suggestions that might add to your pleasure in serving out-of-doors are:

1 Prepare a meal around a main course you select. Barbecue as many other dishes as your time, space, and talent will permit. However, there is no need for every course to be cooked in the great outdoors.

2 If for some reason there is need to delay the serving, plan appetizers that guests can cook on hibachis.

3 Start the fire far enough in advance to be sure the coals will be ready at the desired time.

4 In planning the grocery order be sure to allow for the effect of fresh air on appetites.

5 Keep essential equipment handy — such as, asbestos gloves for handling hot pans or for testing food, tongs for charcoal and another pair for handling food, water pistol or clothes sprinkler to keep flare-ups under control. Don't forget the salt and pepper.

6 Be prepared to move the gathering indoors in the event of rain. Move grill to well ventilated porch, breezeway, or garage.

The combination of congenial friends and good food in a relaxed atmosphere will create an occasion long to be remembered.

BEEF

Any cut of beef can be cooked over hot coals, though the less tender require special preparation—such as marinating or parboiling.

Charcoal Broiled Steak

Best results are achieved by using steaks at least 1½ to 2″ thick and bringing them to room temperature before putting them on the fire. Allow 1 lb. per person of any steak with a bone such as sirloin, porterhouse, club, or T-bone. Half a pound of boneless cuts such as filet is enough for average appetites—if there is such a thing around an open fire.

When serving a small group, choose individual steaks if your grill can accommodate all of them at the same time. Otherwise order one big, very thick steak so that everyone can start the feast at the same time.

Trim off most of the fatty edge. Slash remaining fat at 2″ intervals to prevent curling. Broil over hot fire for 2 min. with the grill close to the fire to seal in juices. Raise grill to 3″ above the fire and continue cooking. When juice comes to top and bubbles on uncooked surface, steak is ready to turn. Turn with tongs (a fork releases juices). Season with salt and pepper. Lower grill and sear second side 2 min. Raise again and complete cooking. (If grill cannot be raised and lowered, arrange grill so heat is 3 to 5″ from steak.) When done to your liking, remove to a big cutting board. Carve the bone out and slice across steak.

When you think the steak is ready, make a slit along the bone with a small, sharp knife and take a look. The following steak timetable may be helpful in planning serving time:

	1″ thick	2″ thick
rare	6 to 8 min. each side	10 to 15 min. each side
medium to well done	10 to 15 min. each side	15 to 20 min. each side

Bleu Cheese Topping for Steak

Combine 1 oz. Bleu or Roquefort cheese with ¼ tsp. Worcestershire sauce; blend well. Spread on top of steak as it comes off the grill. (Bleu cheese lovers spread this on grilled hamburgers, too.)

Broiled Steak with Mushrooms

During the last 10 min. in broiling second side of steak, add mushrooms that have been brushed with butter, turning as needed. Serve broiled mushrooms with steak.

Steak on the Coals

This method startles those who see it for the first time, but it draws ecstatic praise from those who like an emphatic grilled flavor.

Use a large piece of lean, tender steak, such as sirloin, weighing at least 3 lb., 1½ to 2″ thick. Place steak in baking pan and cover with Meat Marinade (recipe below). Refrigerate 3 hr. Turn meat occasionally to thoroughly cover with marinade. Drain steak and allow to come to room temperature.

Have a bed of white-hot charcoal briquets about 3″ deep. A shallow layer of coals will not serve. Remove the grill. Place the meat directly on the fiery coals. Turn every 10 min. to another white-hot area. Allow 12 to 15 min. per side for the center to become rare, hot, and juicy. Allow ½ to ¾ lb. per serving. *Makes 6 servings.*

Meat Marinade: Combine in bowl ½ cup vinegar; ½ cup vegetable oil; 1 small onion, minced; 1 tsp. salt; 1 tsp. dry mustard; ¼ tsp. *each* mace, nutmeg, and cloves; 1 clove garlic, crushed; and ½ tsp. Tabasco. Pour over meat. Serve meat with remaining hot marinade.

Flank Steak Broil

Marinated flank steak charcoal broiled.

Pour Celery-Catsup Marinade (recipe below) over 1 flank steak, about 1½ lb., scored, in shallow baking dish; let stand in refrigerator overnight, spooning sauce over occasionally. Warm to room temperature. Place about 4″ above hot coals. Broil 5 to 7 min ; turn and broil 5 to 7 min. more, or until done. Cut *very thin* slices diagonally *across* the grain. Heat marinade and pass. *6 servings.*

Note: Meat will be pink on the inside.

Celery-Catsup Marinade

⅔ cup catsup
½ cup water
⅓ cup lemon juice
1 tsp. celery seeds
2 tsp. Worcestershire sauce

1 bay leaf
½ tsp. cracked or coarsely
    ground pepper
¼ tsp. crushed basil
dash of Tabasco

Combine all ingredients. Simmer uncovered 10 min. Cool to room temperature.

Grilled Cube Steaks

Inexpensive with no sacrifice of flavor.

Cover 6 cube steaks with California Marinade (recipe below) and let stand 20 min. Put in hinged grill; cook 4 to 5" from coals, about 2 min. on each side, turning as necessary. Season and serve between slices of toast or toasted buns. *6 servings.*

California Marinade

4 cloves garlic, minced
¼ cup olive oil
1 tsp. rosemary, crushed
½ tsp. dry mustard

2 tsp. soy sauce
¼ cup wine vinegar
¼ cup sherry flavoring

Sauté garlic in oil. Add rosemary, mustard, and soy sauce. Remove from heat and stir in vinegar and sherry flavoring.

Swiss Steak Meal in Foil

For each meal:

6 oz. round steak, about
    4x4x1½"
1 tbsp. flour
1 carrot, pared and cut in
    strips
1 small onion, peeled and
    quartered

1 small potato, pared and cut
    in strips
2 green pepper rings
¼ cup chopped celery
2 tbsp. catsup
½ tsp. salt
dash of pepper

Pound flour into steak; place on double thickness of heavy-duty aluminum foil. Arrange carrot, onion, potato, green pepper, and celery on and around steak. Top with catsup, salt, and pepper. Sprinkle with about 1 tbsp. water. Wrap securely. Bake on coals 30 to 40 min., turning every 10 min. to eliminate burning on bottom.

Beef Tenderloin Roast

One of the most delicious of dishes to set before guests, and less expensive than you may guess since it is solid meat and shrinks very little during its relatively short cooking period.

Grill a beef tenderloin (4 to 6 lb.) 4 to 5" from medium coals 15 to 17 min. per side for medium rare or 18 to 23 min. per side for medium. Serve medium rare for best flavor and tenderness. Baste with butter or Tabasco Butter (¼ cup butter and ¼ tsp. Tabasco, blended) throughout the cooking period. *8 to 12 servings.*

Beef Roast on the Turnspit

Wonderful way to serve a large group with a minimum of effort, pictured on page 140.

Select 5 lb. choice rolled rib beef roast. Soak several handfuls of hickory chips in water until saturated and add a little at a time to the fire while charcoaling. Put meat on spit and when juice has sealed itself, baste with Smoky Sauce (recipe below).

medium — roast 2 hr. 15 min. to 2½ hr.
well done — roast 2½ hr. to 3 hr.

Serve extra sauce (double sauce recipe) over roast meat slices. *10 servings.*

Smoky Sauce

2 tbsp. vinegar	1 thin slice lemon
¼ cup water	1 slice peeled onion
1 tsp. brown sugar	2 tbsp. butter
½ tsp. prepared mustard	¼ cup catsup
¼ tsp. pepper	1 tbsp. Worcestershire sauce
¾ tsp. salt	¾ tsp. liquid smoke

Mix vinegar, water, brown sugar, seasonings, lemon, onion, and butter. Bring to boil and simmer 20 min. uncovered. Strain and add remaining ingredients. Heat to boil.

Barbecued Chuck Roast

Meat you will long remember because of flavor and tenderness, pictured on page 138.

Make California Marinade (recipe on p. 79). Place a chuck roast* (3 to 4 lb.), 2½ to 3″ thick, in bowl and pour marinade over. Cover bowl and place in refrigerator. During the next 24 hr. turn meat frequently in marinade. Remove meat and add 2 tbsp. catsup, ½ tsp. Worcestershire sauce, and 1½ tsp. steak sauce to marinade. Stir and apply to meat before barbecuing. Grill 3 to 5″ from coals. Turn meat frequently and baste with hot marinade every 5 to 6 min. Total cooking time will be about 40 min. Serve roast rare in middle and browned on outside. *6 servings.*

*Use U.S. "Choice" grade of meat.

Beef on a Skewer

A meal of meat, fruit, and vegetables—all on a skewer.

Cut 1½ lb. sirloin steak into 1" cubes. Place the beef cubes in Tomato Juice Marinade or Spicy Barbecue Sauce (recipes below) about 2 hr. Wash and prepare ½ lb. mushroom caps; 1 large green pepper, cut in pieces; 1 pt. cherry tomatoes; and ½ fresh pineapple, cut in wedges. Place meat, vegetables, and fruit on skewers. Grill 12 to 15 min. 3 to 5" from coals or until meat is tender. Baste often with sauce. *6 to 8 generous servings.*

***Tomato Juice Marinade*:** Mix 2 cups canned tomato juice, ½ cup vinegar, ¼ cup prepared mustard, 2 tsp. sugar, 2 tsp. salt, and ½ tsp. pepper.

Spicy Barbecue Sauce

½ cup vinegar
½ cup vegetable oil
1 small onion, minced
1 tsp. salt
1 tsp. dry mustard

¼ tsp. *each* mace, nutmeg, cloves
1 clove garlic, crushed
½ tsp. Tabasco

Combine ingredients.

HAMBURGERS

Hamburgers are one of the great favorites of the outdoors, loved by children and grown-ups alike. Lean ground beef gives best results. Ground chuck sold by a reliable meat dealer is less expensive, has even more flavor, and is juicier than ground round. Some homemakers prefer to select a piece of chuck and have it ground adding 2 oz. fat per pound of beef. A pound of ground beef makes 4 thick patties or 8 thin ones.

Double Decker Hamburgers

Everyone's favorite. Set out the thin hamburger patties with a variety of fillings and let guests make their own.

2 lb. ground beef	dash of pepper
2 eggs	½ cup bread crumbs
2 tsp. salt	

Combine ingredients; shape into 20 thin hamburger patties. On half the patties, spread one or more fillings (below), top with remaining thin patties, and seal edges. Place on grill 4 to 6" from hot coals or put in squares of heavy-duty aluminum foil and place directly on top of coals. Cook 15 to 20 min., or until desired doneness. *10 hamburgers.*

Fillings to Mix and Match: Dill pickle slices, pickle relish, prepared mustard, catsup, horse-radish, chopped onions, onion slices, Cheddar cheese slices, pasteurized cheese spread.

Onion Filling: Mix 1 package (1½ oz.) dehydrated onion soup mix with ¼ cup water.

Peppy Cheese Filling: Combine 2 oz. crumbled Bleu cheese or 2 oz. shredded Cheddar cheese with 1 tsp. salt, ¼ tsp. pepper, 2 tbsp. mayonnaise, 1 tsp. Worcestershire sauce, ½ tsp. mustard.

Do-ahead Hamburgers: Add ¼ cup water to 1 package (1½ oz.) dehydrated onion soup mix. Mix with 3 lb. ground chuck. Shape into 12 patties; wrap separately and freeze. Thaw when ready to use.

Barbecued Cheeseburgers in Foil

2 lb. ground beef
1 tsp. salt
⅛ tsp. pepper
1 package (1½ oz.) dehy-
  drated onion soup mix

½ cup water
6 slices processed Cheddar
  cheese

Mix meat and seasonings; shape into 12 patties. Combine soup mix and water to make barbecue sauce; stir until soup is dissolved. Cut heavy-duty aluminum foil into six 10" squares. Place patty in center of each square and spread with onion sauce. Top with cheese slice and second patty. Press edges of hamburgers together. Brush with remaining sauce. Wrap securely. Cook on hot coals 8 to 10 min. per side. Serve on toasted hamburger buns. *6 servings.*

Beefburger Specials

1½ lb. ground beef
¼ cup catsup
1 tbsp. prepared mustard
2 tsp. horse-radish
1 medium onion, finely
  chopped

1½ tsp. salt
¾ cup soft bread crumbs
⅓ cup milk
2 tsp. Worcestershire sauce

Combine all ingredients. Shape into 6 large patties. Broil in folding grill over hot coals about 6 min. on each side until browned outside and medium inside. *6 beefburgers.*

Burger Dogs

A double treat for teens, hamburgers and franks combined.

1 lb. ground beef
2 tbsp. vegetable oil
8 frankfurters, split
  lengthwise

1 can (8 oz.) tomato sauce
1 medium onion, chopped fine
2 tbsp. water
8 frankfurter buns

Brown beef in vegetable oil in heavy skillet over hot coals. Add frank-furters, tomato sauce, onion, and water. Cook about 15 min. Meanwhile, heat buns wrapped in foil. Serve hot mixture on heated buns. *8 servings.*

Asian Hamburger Steaks

Especially popular among grown-ups.

Using 1½ lb. ground beef, make 6 large hamburger patties. Place in oblong pan, 13x9½x2". Pour Asian Sauce (recipe below) over and marinate 2 to 3 hr., turning occasionally. Place in hinged grill about 4 to 5" from hot coals. Grill 8 min. per side for medium or 10 to 12 min. per side for well done. Serve on toasted hamburger buns or with frozen potato balls, wrapped in foil and heated over the coals. *6 servings.*

Asian Sauce: Combine ¼ cup vegetable oil, ¼ cup soy sauce, 2 tbsp. catsup, 1 tbsp. vinegar, ¼ tsp. pepper, and 2 cloves garlic, minced. Mix well.

Charcoal Grilled Meat Loaf

2 lb. ground beef
1 egg
1 medium onion, chopped

½ cup crushed soda crackers
¼ cup catsup
2 tbsp. brown sugar
1 tsp. prepared mustard

Mix beef, egg, onion, and crackers. Add mixture of remaining ingredients; blend well. Lightly grease a 10" skillet. Pat meat into skillet. Space briquets about ½" apart. Place meat loaf on grill 3 to 4" from hot coals. Cook 15 min. Remove from heat. Lay 14" sq. of double thickness heavy-duty aluminum foil on grill and quickly turn meat loaf out onto foil. Brush with Meat Loaf Bar-B-Q Sauce (recipe below). Cook 15 min. longer, or until meat loaf is done. *6 servings.*

Meat Loaf Bar-B-Q Sauce: Combine 3 tbsp. brown sugar, ¼ cup catsup, 1 tsp. dry mustard, and ¼ tsp. nutmeg. Mix well.

FRANKFURTERS

The secret of succulent hot dogs is slow heating—one of the hardest lessons to teach junior cooks whose eager appetites make the necessary minimum of 5 minutes seem like an hour. Children and some adults love to toast their own frankfurters at the end of a stick over hot coals (see picture of Wiener Roast, p. 137) a method that many times produces a hard blackened frank with a tough cold inside. If you are feeding more critical adults, better wrap the franks in flat packages of foil and let them steam.

Tip: Place franks in wide-mouth thermos jug. Fill with boiling water. Screw on cap. The franks will be ready to eat when you arrive at the picnic spot.

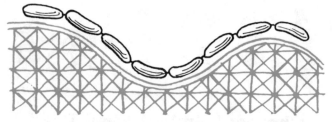

Popular Frankfurter Variations

Coney Islands: Make Coney Sauce (recipe below). Slit 6 franks diagonally; grill over hot coals until brown. Split 6 frankfurter buns; butter, then toast (only an instant). Spoon Coney Sauce generously into each frank-filled roll.

Coney Sauce: Combine and heat 2½ cups chili con carne (1 lb. 4 oz. can), 1 can (6 oz.) tomato paste, 1 tsp. prepared mustard, and ½ tsp. salt.

Stuffed Franks: Split frankfurters lengthwise, almost through. Fill with cheese, thin slice of dill pickle, or peanut butter. Wrap each spirally with strip of bacon, fastening with toothpick at each end. Starting with split side down, grill over hot coals until bacon is crisp. Serve in frankfurter rolls.

Bar-B-Q Franks and Kraut

For each serving, split 2 frankfurters lengthwise. Do not cut through. Spread cut surface of one frankfurter with mustard; spread second frankfurter with catsup. Place 3 to 4 tbsp. drained sauerkraut on one frankfurter; top with second frankfurter and secure ends with toothpicks. Wrap in double thickness of heavy-duty aluminum foil. Place on briquets and cook 3 to 4 min. on each side. Unwrap and serve.

Frank-A-Bobs

Cut each frank into 5 pieces. Alternate on skewer with pineapple chunks; brush with vegetable oil. Broil over hot coals, turning until browned. Serve on toasted frankfurter rolls with mustard or barbecue sauce.

Cheesy Pups

Make Cheese Biscuit Dough (recipe below). Pat dough around franks making a thin covering. Wrap one strip of bacon around dough, securing with toothpicks. Roast over coals or fire.

Cheese Biscuit Dough: Add ⅔ cup milk all at once to 2 cups Bisquick. Stir with fork into a soft dough. Beat dough 15 strokes. It will be stiff and sticky. Stir in ½ cup grated sharp Cheddar cheese. *Covers about 12 franks.*

Barbecued Bologna

Remove outer casing from 2 lb. large bologna, unsliced. With knife, score meat making crisscross cuts, about ½″ apart, just as you would fat on a ham. Stick a whole clove in the center of each diamond. Insert spit rod through center of bologna; tighten skewers at ends to hold meat securely. Broil 5 to 6″ from coals 30 to 40 min., brushing frequently with Chef's Special Sauce (p. 96). *6 servings.*

VEAL

Grilled Veal Chops and Steaks

Don't confuse veal steaks with thick cutlets which are a different cut. Veal sirloin steaks are Porterhouses or T-bones cut from veal instead of beef. This delicate pink meat is a great treat to many people.

Select 1 to 1½" thick veal loin or kidney chops or veal sirloin. Marinate 2 to 3 hr. in soy marinade (described in Katori Meat Kabobs, below). Space hot grey briquets ½" apart. Grease grill and place 3 to 4" above briquets. Grill 8 to 10 min. on each side. *Two chops make 1 serving.*

Mixed Grill combining veal chop with sausage patties or links, broiled bacon, and hot spiced peaches is also delicious.

Katori Meat Kabobs

A specialty of the Far East from your own barbecue grill.

1 cup soy sauce
½ cup sugar
¼ cup vegetable oil
¼ cup sherry flavoring
1 tsp. flavor enhancer
  (monosodium glutamate)

1 clove garlic, chopped
1 lb. veal, cut in 1½" cubes
1 lb. beef tenderloin, cut in
  1½" cubes
1 lb. pork tenderloin, cut in
  1" cubes

Combine soy sauce, sugar, oil, flavoring, flavor enhancer, and garlic. Stir until fully blended. Marinate meat cubes in this mixture for 2 to 3 hr. Alternate marinated meat (6 to 9 cubes per kabob) on skewer, leaving ¼" space between meats. Space briquets in parallel style for kabob cookery. Place kabobs on greased grill about 3 to 4" above briquets. Barbecue 10 to 12 min. on each side, brushing kabobs constantly with marinade. *6 servings.*

Note: Serve with kabobs of vegetables, such as mushrooms, small whole tomatoes, slices of green pepper, small whole onions, or sliced zucchini. Brush with same marinade after vegetables are on skewers.

LAMB

Grilled Lamb Chops

Space briquets ½ to ¾″ apart. Brush grill with vegetable oil. Sear chops 1 to 2 min. Raise grill so chops are 3″ above briquets. Cook until browned. Lower grill and sear second side of chops 1 to 2 min. Raise grill again to 3″ above briquets and grill until chops are done. Season with salt and freshly ground black pepper.

> 1″ chops require 8 min. each side
> 1½″ chops require 10 to 12 min. each side
> 2″ chops require 12 to 15 min. each side

Test for doneness by making slit along side of bone. Meat should be juicy and slightly pink. If desired, lamb chops can be marinated in Spicy Barbecue Sauce (p. 82) and basted with it during last few minutes of cooking.

Note: Flare-ups can be eliminated if aluminum foil drip pan is placed under chops on top of coals. Pan catches drippings from meat.

Rolled Shoulder of Lamb

A less expensive cut than the leg, but just as suitable for spit cooking.

Ask the butcher to bone a 3 to 3½ lb. lamb shoulder, removing as much fat as possible. Spread the meat flat and cover with the following ingredients well mixed:

⅓ cup soft butter
1 clove garlic, crushed
1 tsp. rosemary
1 tsp. salt

½ tsp. pepper
1 cup small bread cubes
1 egg

Roll tightly and tie with string. Fix securely on the turnspit and roast. If desired, baste with vegetable oil or your favorite barbecue sauce. Barbecue 15 to 20 min. per lb. or about 1 hr. Slice to serve. *6 servings.*

Grilled Stuffed Leg of Lamb

Have the butcher remove bone from a leg of lamb without cutting through to the outer surface. Also have removed all but ¼" of the outer fat. For a 7 lb. leg of lamb, prepare the following stuffing:

½ lb. ground raw veal
½ lb. ground precooked ham
½ lb. raw mushrooms,
   chopped fine
½ cup fine soft bread crumbs
1 egg
1 clove garlic, crushed

¼ to ½ tsp. oregano
1 tbsp. Worcestershire sauce
1 tbsp. lemon juice
   (½ lemon)
1 tsp. salt
¼ tsp. pepper

Mix ingredients until smooth and compact. Force tightly into the pocket in the meat. Sew up any openings with heavy-duty string. Wrap in heavy-duty aluminum foil. Place on grill 6 to 8" from hot coals. Turn occasionally during grilling. Allow 20 to 30 min. per lb. or grill until tender and done to your liking. Half hour before ready to serve, remove foil and brown lamb on grill. *6 to 8 servings.*

Marge's Lamb Shish-Kabobs

One of the best ways to serve lamb and vegetables in one dramatic operation, pictured on page 39. So superb that you'll broil them inside often after outdoor dining weather is past.

2 lb. boned lamb shoulder,
   cut into 1½ or 2″ cubes
1 small onion, thinly sliced
2 tsp. salt
¼ tsp. coarsely ground pepper
½ to 1 tsp. oregano

2 medium green peppers,
   cut in pieces
1 fresh pineapple, cubed
1 lb. fresh mushrooms,
   large caps

Place lamb cubes in a bowl. Tuck in onion slices and add seasonings. Refrigerate 1 to 2 hr. To grill, thread cubes of lamb on skewers. Cook 3 to 4″ from hot coals, 15 to 20 min. Remove meat with tongs and alternate on skewer with chunks of green pepper, pineapple cubes, and mushroom caps. (Brush fruits with butter or oil, if desired.) Finish cooking about 15 min., or until meat is done and vegetables and fruit are tender. *4 to 6 servings.*

PORK

Pork requires thorough cooking. Therefore it needs longer grilling than beef or lamb. Barbecued Spareribs are one of the classics of outdoor cookery, but there are dozens of other cuts that lend themselves equally well to the spit or grill.

Barbecued Spareribs

Charcoal flavored ribs with your choice of sauce.

4½ lb. ribs
½ cup soy sauce

1½ tbsp. cornstarch

Place ribs in a large kettle with a cover and add 3 cups of water. Bring to a boil and cook 5 min. Remove ribs from water and drain well. Brush ribs with a mixture of the soy sauce and cornstarch. Continue to brush both sides of ribs, until all the soy-cornstarch mixture is gone. This should be done periodically over a period of 30 to 45 min. to allow the mixture to penetrate into the meat. Place ribs on greased grill about 3″ from briquets. Cook until tender, about 20 min. Every 2 or 3 min. the ribs should be turned and basted each time with Sweet and Sour Sauce or Texas Barbecue Sauce (recipes below). Serve immediately with remaining sauce. *6 servings.*

Sweet and Sour Sauce: Mix 1 cup catsup, 1 cup water, ¼ cup brown sugar (packed), ¼ cup vinegar, ¼ cup Worcestershire sauce, 1 tbsp. celery seeds, 1 tsp. chili powder, 1 tsp. salt, dash of pepper, and few drops Tabasco; bring to boil. Use as basting sauce and serve remainder in individual dishes as a dip for barbecued ribs.

Texas Barbecue Sauce: Mix in saucepan 1 cup tomato juice, ½ cup water, ¼ cup catsup, ¼ cup vinegar, 2 tbsp. Worcestershire sauce, 2 tbsp. brown sugar, 1 tbsp. paprika, 1 tsp. dry mustard, 1 tsp. salt, ¼ tsp. chili powder, and ⅛ tsp. cayenne pepper. Simmer 15 min., or until slightly thickened.

Grilled Pork Chops

Select 1" thick pork loin chops. Bring to room temperature before grilling. Space briquets about ½" apart. Arrange chops on well-greased grill. Sear chops 3 to 4 min. on one side. Raise grill several notches and grill 15 to 18 min. longer. Turn chops and lower grill to sear second side of chops 3 to 4 min. Again raise grill several notches and grill an additional 15 to 20 min., or until done. It is very important that pork be cooked slowly and not too close to the coals, so it is completely cooked. Chops are done when meat loses its pink color throughout. If desired, chops can be brushed with Honey Basting Sauce (recipe below) last few min. of grilling. Serve one chop per person.

Honey Basting Sauce: Combine ¼ cup brown sugar (packed), 2 tbsp. honey, and 1 tbsp. orange juice or other fruit juice; mix thoroughly. Use as a basting sauce for pork or ham steaks. Serve additional sauce with pork chops, if desired.

Charcoal Grilled Pork Tenderloins

This method for barbecuing pork tenderloin seals in the flavorful juices.

Select 1" thick steaks cut from pork tenderloin. Space briquets about ½" apart. Grease grill and place tenderloins on grill. Sear tenderloins 2 to 3 min. on one side. Raise grill 3 to 4" from briquets and barbecue 12 to 15 min. Lower grill and sear second side 2 to 3 min. Raise grill 3 to 4" from briquets and continue to cook until done, 12 to 15 min. Brush meat with Tabasco Butter (¼ cup butter and ¼ tsp. Tabasco, blended) during grilling. Season with salt and pepper. Serve with Caramel Apples (p. 157). Allow 1 to 2 tenderloin steaks per serving.

Note: Cook pork tenderloins slowly until well done. This helps to retain the juice and to make the meat tender.

Pork Teriyaki Barbecue

Flavorful pork grilled until succulent and tender.

Marinate ¼ to ½″ thick slices of fresh pork (pork butt or shoulder) in Teriyaki Sauce (recipe below) overnight in refrigerator. Turn occasionally. Place pork on greased grill 6 to 8″ from hot coals. Turn pork often, about every 3 to 4 min. Grill until pork is tender, 20 to 30 min.

Teriyaki Sauce: Mix ½ cup soy sauce, ¼ cup honey, ½ tsp. flavor enhancer (monosodium glutamate), and 1 clove garlic, minced, or ½ tsp. ginger.

Pork Teriyaki Indoors: Heat oven to 350° (mod.). Place marinated pork on cake rack over pan lined with foil to catch drippings. Bake about 50 min., turning and basting frequently until pork is tender.

Grilled Canadian Bacon and Sausages

Best yet Canadian bacon and sausages to brighten any breakfast. Hearty fare for Breakfast Cookout, pictured on page 144.

1½ lb. unsliced Canadian bacon	½ tsp. hickory smoked salt
¼ cup maple-flavored syrup	⅛ tsp. cloves
	1 pkg. (8 oz.) brown and serve sausages

Make diagonal cuts, ½″ deep at ½″ intervals, in surface of Canadian bacon with a sharp knife. Repeat at an angle to make squares. Combine syrup, salt, and cloves to make a basting sauce. Grill bacon and sausages about 3″ from coals. Baste often with basting sauce. Grill bacon 30 to 45 min., turning often. Grill sausages about 6 min., or until heated through. Serve immediately. *About 8 servings.*

Barbecued Ham on Spit

Use 6 lb. precooked ham for barbecuing, and have the butcher cut it in half diagonally so it can be balanced on the spit.

Remove any rind that is left on ham using a sharp pointed knife. Score fat in a diamond pattern.

Balance two diagonally-cut, precooked ham halves on spit by running spit rod through each half with butt end offset for better balance. Insert spit forks. Tighten fork screws with pliers. Test for balance by rotating spit rod on palms of hands. Insert meat thermometer in center of thickest portion of meat, being sure that it does not rest on bone or fat.

Pile briquets toward back of fire box and knock off grey ash. Place drip pan at front of fire box to catch juices from ham. Attach spit and start motor. Allow 15 to 20 min. per lb. Thermometer will register 170° and ham will pull away from bone. Have extra coals at edge of grill to use as needed.

During last 30 min. of barbecuing, baste with Pineapple Glaze (recipe below).

Pineapple Glaze: Combine 1 can (8 oz.) crushed pineapple or 1 cup pineapple juice, 1 cup brown sugar (packed), 4 tsp. prepared mustard, 2 to 3 tbsp. lemon juice (1 lemon). *Makes about 1½ cups.*

Cinnamon Glazed Ham

For a spur-of-the-moment cookout.

2 to 4 lb. precooked canned ham	⅔ cup honey
	2 tsp. cinnamon

Place ham 6″ from hot coals on greased grill. Turn and baste often with mixture of honey and cinnamon. Grill about 45 min. Serve immediately. *4 to 8 servings.*

Hearty Ham Steak

Appealing barbecued meal when served with Sweet Potato and Pineapple Kabobs (page 128). A "gold mine" recipe—one to be treasured—to be served to everyone, guests and family alike.

Buy 1½ to 2 lb. precooked ham steak, cut about 1" thick. Place on slightly greased grill over hot coals. Baste frequently with heated Chef's Special Sauce (recipe below). Grill 5 to 7 min. per side, until steak is rich brown color. Serve remaining sauce with ham. *About 6 servings.*

Chef's Special Sauce: Mix ¼ cup prepared mustard, ¼ cup pineapple juice, 2 tbsp. sugar, ½ tsp. horse-radish, and dash of salt. Heat.

Grilled Ham Slices

Thick ham slices cut from smoked boneless pork shoulder, basted with Spicy Sizzle Sauce.

Cut a boneless pork shoulder (about 1½ lb.) into ¾" thick slices and marinate in Spicy Sizzle Sauce (recipe below) several hr. Place on grill 4 to 6" from hot coals. Turn and baste often with sauce. Grill about 20 min., or until tender. *8 servings.*

Spicy Sizzle Sauce

1½ cups orange juice*	1 tbsp. dry mustard
½ cup vinegar	1 tbsp. powdered ginger
¼ cup brown sugar (packed)	1 tbsp. molasses
2 tbsp. ground cloves	1 tbsp. brandy flavoring

Combine all ingredients in bowl and mix well with rotary beater.

*Use frozen orange juice, diluted, for quickly prepared juice.

POULTRY

The rotisserie or turnspit are best for whole broiled fowl. Halved or quartered poultry may be barbecued very satisfactorily on the grill. Frequent basting is necessary since most poultry is rather lean. Appetizers of Rumaki (recipe below) make an excellent first course.

Rumaki on the Hibachi

A delectable do-it-yourself chicken liver appetizer for guests to prepare while host or hostess finishes dinner preparation. Pictured on page 139.

6 chicken livers	water chestnuts
6 strips of bacon	brown sugar

Cut chicken livers in half; slice water chestnuts (about 3 slices per nut). Marinate in Teriyaki Sauce (p. 94) for 4 hr. Drain; cut 6 bacon strips in half. Wrap chicken liver pieces and water chestnut in bacon strip. Fasten with toothpick and roll in brown sugar. Arrange appetizers on hibachi over hot coals. Grill until bacon and liver are tender, 15 to 20 min. Turn often. *Makes 12.*

Variation: Appetizers may also be baked in the oven. Place on a wire rack over a shallow roasting pan. Bake at 400° (mod. hot) 20 min., or until bacon is crisp. Turn occasionally for even browning.

Charcoal Grilled Barbecued Chicken

Brush two quartered broiler chickens (1½ to 2 lb.) with Ranch-style Barbecue Sauce (recipe below) or marinate in sauce while getting the fire ready, draining off excess sauce before grilling. Spread hot coals ½" apart with tongs or long stick. Brush grill with fat to keep meat from sticking. Set chicken on grill 6 to 8" from coals. If distance is less, watch carefully to avoid charring. Keep turning chicken every 5 min. basting with sauce, 30 to 60 min., depending on size. *6 to 8 servings.*

Ranch-style Barbecue Sauce

1 cup tomato purée or
   1½ cups tomato juice
½ cup water
⅓ cup lemon juice
¼ cup soft butter
1 medium onion, *finely* chopped

1 tbsp. paprika
1 tbsp. Worcestershire sauce
1 tsp. sugar
1 tsp. salt
½ tsp. pepper

Mix all ingredients and bring just to boil. Keep sauce hot for basting.

Chicken Teriyaki Barbecue

A recipe shared with us by a Japanese-American friend, Mrs. Thomas Oye, Park Ridge, Illinois.

Select a young chicken, not over 2 lb., and cut up into 10 to 12 pieces (breast halves can be cut in half again to make smaller pieces). Marinate in Teriyaki Sauce (p. 94) overnight in refrigerator. Place chicken pieces skin-side-up on greased grill 6 to 8" above hot coals. Turn chicken often, about every 2 min. Grill until chicken is tender, about 30 min. Chicken will be quite dark, but do not be alarmed—this adds to the delicious flavor of the bird.

Barbecued Chicken Halves

A distinctive flavor is imparted by sherry flavoring in the marinade.

Split 3 broiler chickens (about 2 lb. each). Lay flat in 13x9½x2″ pan, pour on California Marinade (p. 79) and let stand 2 to 3 hr. Place chicken halves on greased grill. Turn and baste frequently until done, 30 to 45 min. *6 servings.*

Chipper Chicken

Cut 2 to 3 lb. chicken in pieces. Wash and dry well. Roll chicken pieces in mixture of ¼ cup butter, melted, 1 tsp. garlic salt, 1 tsp. salt, and ⅛ tsp. pepper. Roll in finely crushed potato chips (1 medium bag). Wrap chicken well in foil-covered bowl and take along on picnic.

Lower outdoor grill 2 to 3″ from hot coals. Place chicken in heavy skillet with ½″ hot fat (part butter, if desired). Turn to brown evenly, about 15 min. Raise grill, cover skillet (use tight-fitting lid or aluminum foil), and cook slowly 15 to 20 min. longer. Uncover and cook 5 to 10 min. longer to recrisp.

Note: Take along a deep can to pour the hot grease into when finished frying chicken.

Smothered Chicken

Golden brown chicken in mushroom gravy served with rice will make the family gather in a hurry when you say, "Come and get it."

Dip a broiler chicken (about 2½ lb.), disjointed, in seasoned flour. Place chicken in small amount of butter in iron skillet and set on grill over coals (in lowest position) or on a camp-type gasoline stove. Brown chicken in hot fat; add 1 can (10½ oz.) cream of mushroom soup. Stir in about ¼ cup water or milk. Cover and continue to cook about 30 min. *4 to 6 servings.* For menu including Smothered Chicken, see p. 63.

Success Tip: Add more or less water or milk for desired consistency of gravy.

Chicken on the Spit

Choose two 2 to 2½ lb. broilers. Wash well; dry with paper towels. Rub body cavity of each bird with 2 to 4 tsp. salt and dash of coarsely ground pepper. Arrange chickens on spit rod by inserting rod through body and neck cavity of each bird. Fasten wings to body with skewers. Loop twine around tails and legs, then around spit rod. Tie securely. Insert spit forks into ends of chickens. Test for balance by rotating spit rod in palms of hands. Tighten fork screws. Brush outside surface with vegetable oil.

Knock grey ash from briquets and heap them slightly at rear of fire box. Attach the spit and place drip pan under chicken. Barbecue 2 to 2½ hr., or until leg bone moves easily. Remove chicken and serve immediately. Baste chicken with drippings or butter during last 10 min.

How to make drip pan: Use 4 sheets, about 9″ wide, of heavy-duty aluminum foil. Form an oblong tray, carefully folding corners so drippings won't leak out. Make sides of tray about 1½″ high.

Southern Fried Chicken

Chicken that's crispy on the outside and tender on the inside. Wonderful for picnics, as pictured on page 33.

2½ to 3 lb. frying chicken, cut in pieces	1½ tsp. salt
1 cup GOLD MEDAL Flour	¼ tsp. pepper
	vegetable oil for frying

Place a few chicken pieces in paper bag with flour, salt, and pepper. Shake well to coat chicken. Remove. Repeat until all chicken is coated. Starting with meaty pieces, place chicken in heavy skillet in hot vegetable oil, ½ to 1″ deep. Cover; cook 10 to 15 min. over medium heat. Remove cover, reduce heat and keep turning chicken until all pieces are uniformly browned, 20 to 25 min. Drain on absorbent paper. Serve hot with Hush Puppies (p. 151) or fill a pan with chicken, cover well with foil, wrap in newspaper, or place in insulated bag and take along on picnic.

Game Hens on the Spit

Place ¼ small apple and ¼ small onion in cavity of each 14 to 16 oz. Rock Cornish game hen. Season cavity generously with salt and pepper. Skewer and lace cavity shut. Arrange several game hens on spit. Check for balance. Baste with Tabasco Butter (½ tsp. Tabasco blended with ½ cup butter) throughout cooking period. Cook about 50 min., or until tender. *1 game hen per serving.*

Grilled Game Hens: Prepare game hens (above)—*except* cook skin-side-down on greased grill 4″ from coals 25 to 30 min. or until golden brown and tender, turning twice and basting often.

Whole Barbecued Turkey

Simplest way to entertain a large group of friends. Pictured on page 35.

Use a vented grill with closely fitting cover for that charcoal-grilled flavor.

Rub body cavity of 20 lb. turkey with mixture of ¼ cup salt and ½ tsp. Tabasco; rub neck cavity with mixture of 2 tbsp. salt and few drops Tabasco. Place 2 apples, quartered, and 2 onions, quartered, in body cavity. Fasten large opening with skewers and lace shut. Tie leg ends to tail. Fasten neck skin to back with skewers. Lift wing tip up and over back for natural brace when turned over. Brush with unsalted fat or vegetable oil. Place bird in shallow pan and brown on both sides. Place cover over turkey leaving vent open and adjust dampers. Cook 15 min. per lb. or about 5 hr. basting occasionally with turkey drippings. Let the bird rest in a warm place for 15 min. before carving to make carving easier and retain juices in meat.

Note: Roast smaller turkeys 20 min. per lb. For a 10 lb. turkey, you'll need 2 tbsp. salt and ¼ tsp. Tabasco for body cavity and 1 tbsp. salt and 2 drops Tabasco for neck cavity.

FISH AND SHELLFISH

Charcoal broiled fish is a prime treat if the easy rules for its cooking are observed. Fish has little fat and so needs constant basting. The meat is delicate and should be broiled only until it loses its transparent look. Overcooked fish tends to fall apart and to be dry. A two-sided grill is almost an essential in the handling of any but large whole fish. They need a different treatment. Allow 1 lb. of fish per person.

Fried Fish

Most campers claim, and with some reason, that there is nothing so good as a fresh-caught fish sizzled to a crisp golden brown in a skillet over a glowing fire on the shore. Try this for small game fish such as trout, perch, sunfish, and crappies.

Scale and clean fish. Remove head if you wish. Sprinkle with salt and pepper. Dip in flour or corn meal. Pan-fry in heavy cast-iron skillet with fat ⅛″ deep (part butter gives superb flavor) on grill 4 to 5″ from coals until golden brown. Turn carefully and brown on other side, cooking about 10 min. in all. Be sure not to crowd fish in the pan. Drain on absorbent paper. Serve hot with lemon wedges.

Sometime when you have many small whole fish you may want to cook them over the campfire as the children of one of my friends delight in doing. Clean fish but leave heads and tails on. Run a peeled green switch or a long skewer through the mouth and out at the tail. Roll the fish in salted oil or melted butter and cook over the fire, turning often just as you would wieners on a stick.

Barbecued Fish Fillets

Fillets brushed with a delicious butter sauce.

Clean and fillet a fish (bass, pike, mackerel, trout) weighing about 3 lb. Wash and dry well. Brush with vegetable oil and place in hinged grill or on well-greased grill. Barbecue 3 to 4″ from coals about 5 min. per side, or until fish tests done. Brush often with melted Lemon Butter (add ¼ cup lemon juice to ½ cup butter, melted). Just before serving sprinkle with salt and pepper.

How to clean and fillet fish: Hold fish by the tail. Scrape with a blunt knife (or fish scraper) from tail to head in short, firm strokes. Slit underside, remove entrails. Cut down the back of fish from head to tail on either side of and close to backbone. Cut the flesh free from the rib bones. Skin fish, if desired, beginning at tail end. Remove scales before filleting fish.

Scallop Kabobs

1 lb. scallops, fresh or frozen
1 can (4 oz.) button
    mushrooms, drained
1 can (13½ oz.) pineapple
    chunks, drained
¼ cup vegetable oil

¼ cup soy sauce
¼ cup lemon juice
¼ cup chopped parsley
½ tsp. salt
dash of pepper
12 slices bacon

Thaw frozen scallops. Remove any shell particles and wash. Place mushrooms, pineapple, and scallops in bowl. Combine vegetable oil, soy sauce, lemon juice, parsley, salt, and pepper. Pour sauce over scallop mixture and let stand 30 min., turning once.

Fry bacon slowly until cooked but not crisp. Cut each slice in half. Alternate scallops, mushrooms, pineapple, and bacon on long metal skewers. Place on grill about 4″ from hot coals. Cook 6 min. Turn and cook about 6 min. longer. *4 servings.*

Shrimp Boil

On a hot summer day, zesty shrimp on a platter of cracked ice served with crackers and pitchers of iced tea is very refreshing. Pictured on page 139.

4 qt. water
6 cups diced celery
2 cups chopped onion
4 lemons, quartered
4 cloves garlic, minced
12 bay leaves

6 tbsp. salt
2 tbsp. whole allspice
4 tsp. cayenne pepper
6 lb. headless shrimp (with
    shells still on)

Bring water to boil in large kettle. Add all ingredients except shrimp. Simmer 15 min. Add shrimp; heat to boil; simmer 15 min. Remove from heat. Let shrimp stand 20 min. in shrimp boil; drain. Serve on platter of cracked ice with favorite cocktail or horse-radish sauce. *6 main dish servings; 12 to 16 appetizer servings.* Cut recipe in half for 6 to 8 appetizer servings.

Shrimp Carmel

½ cup butter
2 tsp. garlic salt
⅛ tsp. Tabasco
3 lb. frozen shelled,
    deveined shrimp, thawed
2 cans (4 oz. each) water
    chestnuts, drained and
    sliced

1 large green pepper, cut in
    rings
1 tbsp. minced onion
½ tsp. salt
½ tsp. dried tarragon

Prepare a foil pan made from several large pieces of heavy-duty aluminum foil, at least ½″ deep. Place butter, garlic salt, and Tabasco in foil pan and set on kettle grill (grill with cover) or on open grill (grill without cover). Add shrimp and remaining ingredients. Place cover on kettle grill, adjust dampers and vents; cook 20 to 30 min. Or cover pan with foil and seal edges well. Grill 6 to 8″ from heat 20 to 30 min. Serve immediately. *About 6 servings.*

Shrimp en Brochette

1 lb. fresh or frozen shrimp,
    cooked
½ lb. bacon

¼ cup butter
¼ cup lemon juice
    (about 2 lemons)

Peel and devein shrimp, if necessary. Wrap ½ slice bacon around each shrimp. Secure with wooden pick. (If small shrimp are used, it may be possible to wrap two or three at one time. Then allow one whole strip of bacon for wrapping.) Combine butter and lemon juice in small saucepan. Stir over low heat until butter melts. Grill on hibachi or outdoor grill about 3″ from coals. Turn and baste often with lemon butter. Grilling time is about 15 min., or until bacon is crisp and brown. *Makes 12 to 16 appetizers.*

Crispy Fried Shrimp

Dip 1½ lb. deveined fresh shrimp in Dipping Batter (recipe below). Shallow fry in hot oil (1″ deep) in large, heavy skillet over hot coals 5 to 10 min., or until golden brown and crisp. Hush Puppies (p. 151) and onion rings may be fried right along with shrimp. Serve with Biloxi Dip (recipe below). *About 6 servings.*

Dipping Batter

1 cup *sifted* GOLD MEDAL Flour	1 egg, slightly beaten
½ tsp. salt	¼ cup vegetable oil
1 tsp. baking powder	1 cup milk

Sift flour, salt, and baking powder together. Mix egg, oil, and milk; add to dry ingredients. Beat with rotary beater until smooth. Coat food to be fried with unseasoned flour or corn meal. Dip into batter. Drain. Fry.

Biloxi Dip

Mix well ½ cup catsup, 2 tbsp. lemon juice, 2 tbsp. vegetable oil, ½ tsp. grated lemon rind, ½ tsp. horse-radish, and dash of Tabasco. *Makes about ¾ cup.*

Whole Stuffed Barbecued Fish

Charcoal grilling makes fish a superb cookout delicacy.

Scale and clean an 8 to 10 lb. fish (tuna, salmon, pike, bass) as described on p. 103. Wash and wipe out well. Cut out backbone with scissors to within 2″ of tail. Sprinkle the cavity with salt and pepper. Stuff fish with Garden Vegetable Stuffing (recipe below). Fasten opening with skewers; lace shut. Brush the outside skin with vegetable oil. Place fish in wire basket or bind fish in a piece of chicken wire large enough to wrap around it. (You will need wire snippers and a pair of pliers to open this homemade rack later.) Lay fish on grill 4 to 6″ from the hot coals. Baste often with a combination of melted butter and lemon juice. Grill fish 45 min., turning 3 times, or until fish tests done. *About 12 servings.*

Garden Vegetable Stuffing

2 cups dry bread cubes	1½ tbsp. lemon juice
1 cup coarsely grated raw carrot	(½ lemon)
	1 egg
1 cup finely chopped onion, sautéed in butter	1 clove garlic, minced
	2 tsp. salt
1 cup chopped raw mushrooms	¼ tsp. marjoram
	¼ tsp. pepper
½ cup chopped parsley	

Combine all ingredients and mix well. Wrap remaining stuffing in foil and set on grill beside fish. Heat through.

Note: 2 to 4 day old bread is best for stuffing.

Fish Steaks

Large, firm-fleshed fish steaks brushed with Lemon-Parsley Butter.

Cut steaks of salmon, tuna, halibut, swordfish, or any other large, firm-fleshed fish 1 or 1½″ thick or thaw frozen fish steaks. Dip in melted butter. Arrange in a long-handled, hinged grill. Sprinkle with salt and pepper. Grill 5 to 7 min. per side or until knife test shows that center has lost its transparency. Baste often with Lemon-Parsley Butter (recipe below). Do not overcook. Serve with remaining butter sauce. Allow 1 fish steak per serving.

Lemon-Parsley Butter: Melt ½ cup butter in saucepan. Add ¼ cup lemon juice and 1½ tbsp. finely cut parsley.

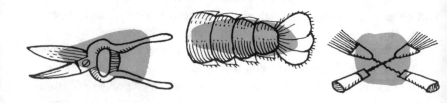

Grilled Lobster Tails

Thaw six large lobster tails. Cut through lobster shell on top and under-side lengthwise with kitchen shears. Brush grids on outdoor grill lightly with fat. Place lobster tails, under-side-down, on grill. Cook 5 min., or until meat is brown. Turn and brush with Lemon Butter Sauce (recipe below). Cook 15 to 20 min. longer. Continue brushing with hot sauce throughout cooking period. Serve with remaining sauce. *6 servings.*

Lemon Butter Sauce

½ cup butter	1 tbsp. chopped parsley
1 tbsp. lemon juice	¼ to ½ tsp. Tabasco

Combine ingredients and cook over low heat until butter is melted. Keep butter sauce warm while brushing lobster.

Steamed Clams

A favorite wherever fresh clams are available.

You will need a deep kettle with a tight-fitting lid for this.

Scrub shells. Discard any that are open. Add 1″ water to kettle with clams. Cover tightly and steam only until the shells open, 10 min. Serve on big plates, discarding any unopened clams. On the side, serve each guest a bowl of the hot clam broth from the bottom of the kettle and another bowl of melted butter. Clams are dunked first into broth to remove any sand and then into the butter for seasonings. *6 lb. of clams serves 6.*

Broiled Lobster

Broiled deep-sea lobster, grilled to a juicy tenderness with melted butter.

You need live lobsters for this. Shortly before grilling, place lobster on its back. With sharp knife, split open from head to tail; cut off membrane using knife or lobster shears. Remove black vein or intestinal tract, running from head to tail. Remove stomach or "lady" located at the back of the head. Save the soft green parts (the liver) and the coral (the roe). Brush body, shell, and claws thoroughly with oil. (This keeps them from looking dry and crusty.) Place lobsters on grill, shell-side-down. Brush meat liberally with salted butter. Grill over low heat, until the meat loses its transparent look. A hot fire will burn the claws before the tail meat is cooked. Do not turn or you will lose the luscious juice collected in the shell. Serve with melted butter and lemon wedges and plenty of paper napkins.

Note: A 1 to 2½ lb. lobster will be done in 15 to 18 min.

Broiled Stuffed Lobster: Follow recipe above—except for each lobster mix the liver and the roe with 2 tbsp. dry bread crumbs, ¼ tsp. Worcestershire sauce, and 1 tsp. chopped parsley and stuff in cavity.

Success Tip: Live lobsters can be kept in your refrigerator up to 3 days. Don't try to keep them alive by running under fresh water as this will suffocate them.

New England Clam Chowder

1 pt. clams	1 cup diced potatoes
¼ cup chopped bacon or salt pork	½ tsp. salt
	dash pepper
¼ cup chopped onion	2 cups milk
1 cup clam liquor and water	parsley

Drain clams and save liquor. Chop. Fry bacon until light brown. Add onion and cook until tender. Add liquor, potatoes, seasonings, and clams. Cook about 15 min., or until potatoes are tender. Add milk; heat. Garnish with chopped parsley sprinkled over the top. *6 servings.*

Bouillabaisse

Rich fish soup of French origin just filled with large pieces of fish, shrimp, lobster, clams, and simmered in a full-flavored tomato broth.

1 cup chopped onion	6 frozen lobster tails, thawed and cut in half, lengthwise
¼ cup diced carrot	
1 clove garlic, minced	1 lb. shrimp
½ cup vegetable oil	1 can (10½ oz.) whole clams (do not drain)
3 lb. frozen fish fillets, such as pike, thawed and cut in 3″ pieces	
	1 can (10½ oz.) bouillion
2 cups (16 or 17 oz. can) whole tomatoes	½ cup diced pimiento
	¼ cup chopped parsley
2 bay leaves, crushed	1 tbsp. lemon juice
2 qt. water	1 tbsp. salt
	½ tsp. saffron
	dash freshly ground pepper

In large kettle, sauté onion, carrot, and garlic in vegetable oil until onion is transparent, about 10 min. Add fish fillets, tomatoes, bay leaves, and water. Bring to boil; reduce heat. Simmer gently 30 min. Add remaining ingredients and simmer gently an additional 30 min. Serve piping hot in large soup bowls with French bread to absorb broth. *About 12 servings.*

ONE DISH DINNERS

Dinners-in-a-dish, skillet main dishes, meals-in-foil, hearty sandwiches, and stews combine with salad and dessert for speedy yet satisfying meals while traveling or camping out.

Dinner-in-a-Can

A tasty dinner cooked in one-pound coffee cans. Good for "Hobo" parties or for out-in-the-woods meals.

1 lb. ground meat (meat loaf
   mixture with pork)
2 carrots
4 tomatoes

1 can (1 lb. 13 oz.) whole
   kernel corn, drained
Bisquick Dumplings
   (recipe below)

Season meat as desired and divide into 4 patties. Grease four 1 lb. coffee cans. Place a meat patty in bottom of each can. On top of patty place 3 or 4 thin strips of carrot, 3 slices of tomato, and ¼ of corn. Dot with butter. Season with salt and pepper. Cover securely. Place on grill; cook 20 to 30 min. Drop small spoonfuls of Dumpling batter on each. Sprinkle with minced parsley or chives. Cover and cook 15 to 20 min. longer. *4 average servings.*

Bisquick Dumplings: Mix 1 cup Bisquick and ⅜ cup (¼ cup plus 2 tbsp.) milk thoroughly.

Pocket Stew

Called Pocket Stew because hikers carry ingredients and utensils in their pockets for the noon meal.

Make 4 hamburger patties from 1 lb. ground beef. Place each patty on 12″ sq. of double thickness heavy-duty aluminum foil. Top with slice of onion and slice of raw potato. Add two carrot strips. Sprinkle with 1 tsp. salt and ⅛ tsp. pepper. Seal foil securely. Place in hot coals 25 min., turning twice during cooking. *4 servings.*

Chicken Jambalaya

3 lb. fryer, cut in pieces
½ lb. ham, cubed
3 tbsp. vegetable oil
1 cup chopped green pepper
   (1 large)
1 cup chopped onion (1 large)
1 clove garlic, minced

2 tsp. Worcestershire sauce
¼ tsp. thyme
¼ tsp. Tabasco
¼ tsp. black pepper
3 cups hot water
1½ cups uncooked rice

Brown chicken and ham in oil. Remove meat. Sauté pepper, onion, and garlic 5 min. over low heat. Add seasonings and water. Simmer 10 min. Add rice and meat. Cover and cook over low heat 25 min. Fluff rice with fork and cook 5 min. longer. *8 servings.*

Sea Food Jambalaya: Follow directions for Chicken Jambalaya—except substitute 12 oz. frozen oysters, thawed, and 1 lb. peeled, cooked shrimp for chicken. For menu featuring Sea Food Jambalaya, turn to p. 60.

Veal Scallopini

1 clove garlic
1½ lb. veal, cut thin and in
   serving pieces
¼ cup vegetable oil
¾ cup sliced onion
1 can (4 oz.) mushrooms, drained

2 tbsp. flour
½ tsp. salt
⅛ tsp. pepper
½ cup water
1 cup tomato sauce

Cook garlic and meat in oil until meat is brown. Remove meat and discard garlic. Cook onions and mushrooms in oil until tender. Blend in flour, salt, and pepper; let bubble. Gradually stir in water and tomato sauce; cook until thickened, stirring constantly. Add browned meat and cook 10 min. Sprinkle with Parmesan cheese. *4 to 6 servings.* For menu featuring Veal Scallopini, turn to p. 63.

Tagliarini

Hearty Italian skillet dish with noodles, meat, tomatoes, corn, and olives.

3 tbsp. olive oil
1 lb. ground beef
1½ tsp. salt
⅛ tsp. black pepper
few grains cayenne pepper
1 tsp. oregano
1 medium onion, chopped
  (about ¾ cup)
1 clove garlic, minced
1 medium green pepper, chopped
  (about ¾ cup)

2 cans (1 lb. each) Italian-style
  tomatoes
1 can (10 oz.) whole kernel
  corn with liquid
1 can (7 oz.) pitted ripe olives,
  drained
4 oz. (1½ cups) noodles,
  uncooked
¼ to ½ cup grated Parmesan
  cheese or 1 cup grated sharp
  Cheddar cheese (¼ lb.)

Heat olive oil in large heavy skillet. Brown meat. Add remaining ingredients except cheese and cook covered over low heat, stirring occasionally, about 25 min. Remove lid from skillet and cook another 10 to 15 min. If Parmesan cheese is used, remove to serving dish and sprinkle with cheese, serving additional cheese, if desired. If Cheddar cheese is used, fold carefully into the mixture and serve. *8 generous servings.*

Harvest Corn

4 slices bacon
1 medium green pepper,
  chopped
1 small onion, chopped

2 cups cream-style corn
  (16 oz. can)
1 tsp. salt
⅛ tsp. pepper
4 eggs, beaten

Fry bacon until crisp. Remove from skillet; drain off most of fat. Sauté green pepper and onion in remaining fat for 5 min. Stir in corn, salt, pepper, and eggs. Stir until eggs are set. Add bacon, broken into small pieces. *4 to 6 servings.*

Potato-Egg Scramble

Dice 4 boiled medium potatoes. Dice 6 slices bacon and fry until crisp;
pour off half the fat. Add potatoes and onions (1 bunch green onions,
chopped). Fry until lightly browned. Add 4 eggs. Season with salt and
pepper. Stir gently until eggs are set. *4 servings.*

Meat Balls with Puff Biscuits

One-dish meal that is sure to please. See picture on page 40.

1 lb. ground beef	Biscuit Balls (recipe below)
½ lb. ground pork	1½ tsp. oregano
1 egg, slightly beaten	1 tsp. paprika
1 tsp. salt	1 large green pepper, chopped
⅛ tsp. pepper	1 large onion, chopped
1 tbsp. fat	2 cans (8 oz. each) tomato
	sauce

Mix meats, egg, salt, and pepper. Shape into 12 small hamburger
patties. Brown in hot fat in skillet on grill or camp stove. While meat
is browning, shape biscuits into balls. Roll in mixture of oregano and
paprika. When meat is browned, drain off excess fat. Add green pepper,
onion, and tomato sauce. Arrange biscuits on top of hamburger patties.
Cover tightly; cook over medium heat 20 min., or until biscuits are
done (to test, break in center with fork).

Biscuit Balls: Mix 1 cup Bisquick and ⅓ cup milk thoroughly. Roll
out about ½″ thick; shape into 10 or 12 balls.

Note: Biscuits may be rolled in oregano and paprika before they are
taken out to the grill. Sauce ingredients may be combined ahead of time.

Submarines

Big, hearty sandwiches of meat and cheese, pictured on page 36.

2 loaves long French bread or
  6 individual loaves French
  bread
six ¼" thick slices boiled ham
  (about 1 lb.)

six ¼" thick slices salami
  (about 1¼ lb.)
1 pkg. (8 oz.) sliced Swiss
  cheese
1 pkg. (8 oz.) sliced Cheddar
  cheese

Cut long French bread loaves into thirds. Split each third in two, horizontally, and spread with butter. Place one slice of each kind of meat and each kind of cheese between bread slices. Spoon some Favorite Barbecue Sauce (recipe below) over sandwich fillings. Wrap individual servings securely in single layer of heavy-duty foil. Place on grill 3 to 4" from briquets or in 350° (mod.) oven until cheese melts, about 15 min. Serve with several platters of different accompaniments such as lettuce, sliced tomatoes, sliced onion, sliced pickles, sweet pickle relish, olives, mayonnaise, catsup, mustard, and hot Barbecue Sauce. *6 servings.*

Favorite Barbecue Sauce

1 cup catsup
¾ cup chili sauce
¾ cup brown sugar (packed)
¾ cup wine vinegar
¼ cup vegetable oil
½ cup lemon juice
3 tbsp. steak sauce

2 tbsp. Worcestershire sauce
2 tbsp. dry mustard
1 tbsp. soy sauce
1 tbsp. freshly ground
  black pepper
2 cloves garlic, minced

Combine all ingredients except garlic and mix well. About 1 hr. before using sauce, add garlic. Heat and serve as an accompaniment to sandwiches. Store remaining sauce in refrigerator. *Makes about 4½ cups.*

Stews

Call it mulligan, ragout, slumgullion, or burgoo—good old stew is one of the best ways to keep a hungry crowd coming happily back for more. Stews are beloved by camp cooks because, once started, they demand little attention. Stewing is the safest way to treat tougher cuts, as all hunters know, but is equally good with tender young rabbit, squirrel, chicken, lamb, or veal. Either fresh or dried vegetables go well, and dumplings may be added to make stew truly a complete one-pot meal.

Brunswick Stew

3 lb. stewing hen, cut up
1½ tsp. salt
¼ lb. salt pork, cut in 1" pieces
4 cups tomatoes, peeled and
thickly sliced
2 cups fresh cut corn
1 cup coarsely chopped
potatoes

1 pkg. (10 oz.) Lima beans,
frozen
½ cup chopped onion
(1 small)
1 tsp. salt
¼ tsp. pepper
dash of cayenne pepper

Place chicken in large heavy kettle or Dutch oven with just enough water to cover. Add 1½ tsp. salt. Cover. Simmer gently until tender, about 2 hr. Add more water if necessary. Add vegetables and seasonings. Simmer slowly until soup is thick and well blended, about 2 hr. *8 to 10 servings.*

Note: If toting canned goods, substitute canned vegetables for fresh in these amounts: two cans (16 or 17 oz. each) tomatoes, 1 can (16 or 17 oz.) whole kernel corn, 1 can (16 or 17 oz.) whole new potatoes. Include the vegetable liquid, too.

Note: Flavor improves if stew is refrigerated and reheated. May be made in advance and frozen.

Lamb Stew with Parsley Dumplings

2 lb. boneless lamb shoulder,
    cut in 2" cubes
2 cups hot water
2 tsp. salt
¼ tsp. pepper
1 small bay leaf

3 medium carrots, cut in 1" pieces
1 medium onion, sliced
1 medium potato, diced, or
    1 turnip, diced
1 cup fresh or frozen peas

Brown meat in 2 tbsp. hot fat over medium heat in Dutch oven. Add water and seasoning. Simmer covered 2 hr., adding more water, if needed. Add carrots, onion, and potato; cook over medium heat 20 min. Add peas. Thicken stew and top with Parsley Dumplings (recipe below). *6 servings.*

Parsley Dumplings: Add ¾ cup milk and ¼ cup chopped parsley to 2 cups Bisquick. Mix thoroughly with fork. Drop by spoonfuls onto boiling stew. Cook over low heat 10 min. uncovered and 10 min. covered. Liquid should just bubble gently.

Kentucky Burgoo

One taste of this appetizing concoction of beef, veal, chicken, and vegetables makes a burgoo fan of anyone. The early pioneers in Kentucky found pleasure and excitement in burgoo and barbecue feasts and the practice became an institution.

4 to 5 lb. stewing hen
1 lb. stewing beef, cut in
   2″ pieces
1 lb. veal shoulder, cut in
   2″ pieces
3 qt. water
1 lb. small white potatoes,
   halved
1 lb. small white onions,
   halved
2 cups carrots, chopped
3 cups celery, chopped
2 medium green peppers,
   chopped
1 pkg. (10 oz.) frozen Lima
   beans

2 cups okra, whole or diced
2 cups whole kernel corn
   (16 or 17 oz. can), drained
2 cups tomatoes
   (16 or 17 oz. can)
1 cup tomato purée
   (10½ oz. can)
2 tbsp. salt (add more, if
   desired)
1 tsp. pepper
1½ tsp. dry mustard
1 tsp. chili powder
¼ tsp. Tabasco
⅛ tsp. cayenne pepper
½ cup chopped parsley,
   if desired

Combine meats and water in large heavy kettle (about 8 qt.). Cover; cook over low heat until tender (2 to 3 hr.). Remove meats. Skim off excess fat. Remove skin from chicken; separate from bones and cut up coarsely. Replace meats in stock. Add vegetables and salt. Simmer until flavors are well-blended, 2½ to 3 hr. Add remaining seasonings. Just before serving, add chopped parsley. Serve with crisp hot bread or biscuits. *15 to 20 servings*.

Note: Flavor improves if stew is refrigerated and reheated. May be made in advance and frozen.

VEGETABLES

As do so many other foods, vegetables take on a new allure when barbecued. If you are having trouble getting your family to even look at vegetables, try the following recipes—and see the vegetables (and their valuable vitamins) eaten with pleasure.

Green Beans with Mushrooms and Onions

Green beans as you'll like them.

1 pkg. (12 oz.) frozen French
    cut green beans
1 can (3 to 4 oz.) sliced
    mushrooms, drained
2 tbsp. butter

salt and pepper
1 pkg. frozen French fried
    onions or ½ can (3¼ oz.)
    French fried onions

Place beans on double thickness of heavy-duty aluminum foil. Add mushrooms, butter, salt, and pepper. Wrap food securely in foil. Barbecue on coals 10 to 20 min., or on grill 30 to 40 min., turning 2 or 3 times. To serve, place in serving dish and distribute mushrooms evenly throughout beans. Place onions on beans; serve immediately. *6 servings.*

Note: Warmth of beans will heat canned onions. If using frozen onions, place on foil and heat at edges of grill before placing on top of beans.

Speedy Baked Beans

Ideal for camping trips or wiener roasts. Pictured on page 137.

4 strips bacon, diced
1 large onion, minced
2 cans (1 lb. 4 oz. each)
 baked beans (with pork)

1 tsp. prepared mustard
¼ cup chili sauce

Heat oven to 350° (mod.). Sauté bacon and onion until bacon is crisp and onion yellow. Stir in the beans, mustard, and chili sauce. Pour into greased 1½-qt. baking dish. Bake 45 min. uncovered, until beans are brown and bubbly. Serve hot. *6 servings.*

Outdoor Creamy Cabbage

Entirely different flavor from cabbage cooked any other way.

Cut 10" squares of aluminum foil. Chop cabbage; place individual serving (about 1 cup raw cabbage) on foil squares. Bring 2 ends together folding sides securely, thus leaving top open to form cup. Pour in 1 tbsp. cream, season with salt and pepper, dot with ½ tbsp. butter. Fold top edges over securely to hold in steam. Place on grill about 4" from hot coals. Grill about 30 min.

Grilled Sweet Carrot Sticks

8 to 10 large carrots
2 tbsp. butter

salt and pepper
¼ cup brown sugar (packed)

Clean and pare carrots. Cut carrots into strips. Place on double thickness of heavy-duty aluminum foil. Add butter, salt, and pepper. Wrap very securely in foil. Barbecue 1 hr. on grill or 30 to 40 min. on briquets. Just before serving, sprinkle brown sugar over carrots. Heat of carrots will melt the brown sugar. *6 servings.*

Note: If desired, honey may be substituted for brown sugar.

Herb-seasoned Charcoal Grilled Carrots: Follow recipe above—except before wrapping, sprinkle carrots lightly with dill weed or thyme. Omit brown sugar.

Roast Corn

This is a universal favorite. Properly cooked, corn is almost a meal in itself, since no one ever seems to get enough or to tire of it during its brief season. Get young tender corn straight from the field if you possibly can. Serve with plenty of butter, salt, and paper napkins.

Corn Roasted on Grill over Coals

Remove large outer husks from young tender corn; turn back inner husks, remove silk. Spread corn with softened butter. Pull husks back over ears, tying with fine wire. Roast on grill over hot coals, turning frequently until done, 20 to 30 min. Serve at once with salt, pepper, and more butter.

Corn Roasted in Foil on Coals

With Husks: Follow directions above—except rewrap corn in husks, then in heavy-duty aluminum foil. Lay on ash-grey coals 20 to 30 min., turning once.

Without Husks: Remove husks and silk. Place on piece of heavy-duty aluminum foil. Add 1 tbsp. butter and 1 ice cube (or about 2 tbsp. water). Wrap securely; lay on ash-grey coals 20 to 30 min., turning once.

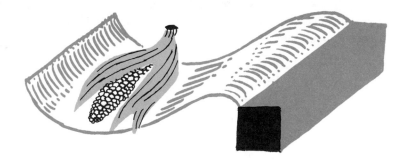

Eggplant Italian-style

Eggplant with a difference—grilled with onion and Mozzarella cheese.

Peel eggplant. Cut in 1½″ rounds. Put on pieces of aluminum foil. Season with salt, white pepper, and oregano. Add a big round of Bermuda onion, ¼″ thick, and a slice of Mozzarella cheese, ¼″ thick. Add ½ tomato, cut-side-up, sprinkled with salt and rosemary and dotted with butter. Seal tightly in foil and cook on grill about 30 min., or until eggplant is soft.

Note: Use oregano and rosemary sparingly. Use plenty of Mozzarella cheese.

Foil-grilled Peppers

Hot baked green peppers stuffed with chili beans.

6 medium green peppers   ¾ cup catsup
1 can (15 oz.) chili beans,
   drained

Clean green peppers for stuffing. Place each on a double thickness of heavy-duty aluminum foil. Place 1 tbsp. catsup in each green pepper. Fill centers with chili beans. Top each green pepper with another tablespoonful of catsup. Wrap securely in foil. Cook on briquets 15 to 20 min., turning occasionally, or on grill 3 to 4″ from heat 30 to 40 min. (turn once). *6 servings.*

Variations: a.   Follow recipe above—except add ½ cup whole kernel corn.

              b.   Fill center of peppers with 1 can Spanish rice instead of chili beans and catsup. Salt and pepper to taste.

Note: Do not overcook, as green peppers will become soggy.

Roast Onions

There are two good ways to cook whole onions on an open fire that are supremely good and easy—and that give them a taste so different from those done in the kitchen that they seem almost like another vegetable.

Roasted Bermuda Onions

Choose big ones of even size (one for each person). Place them directly on the grill over a hot fire, or nestle them in the coals at the edge. They will sizzle and snap and send off a delicious aroma. The outside chars to a thick black crust, but don't worry. The inside heart is steaming. Use tongs to turn. To test for doneness squeeze lightly with your grilling mitts. When they have cooked 30 to 45 min. and are soft, they are ready. With grilling mitts, grasp the blackened crust and squeeze out the golden heart. The inner layers will be dark yellow, sweeter than any onion you have ever tasted and perfumed with concentrated juices and smoke.

Onions Roasted in Foil

Cut off tops of 6 medium onions to remove stem ends. Make 4 cuts halfway through each onion. Place onion on a sq. of heavy-duty aluminum foil large enough to cover the onion. Pour ½ tsp. Worcestershire sauce over the top of the onion or brush top with liquid smoke. Fold foil securely around onion. Roast on coals about 30 min., on grill 45 min. to 1 hr., turning at 10 min. intervals. Test for doneness by squeezing the packet with tongs or hands encased in grilling mitts. To serve, remove outer skin of onion. *6 servings.*

French Fried Onion Rings

Cut onions into ¼″ slices and separate into rings. Dry onions thoroughly, then coat generously with flour. Dip into Dipping Batter (recipe below), letting excess drain off. Fry until brown in hot oil ½ to 1″ deep in skillet on grill over hot coals. *Three large onions will make 6 servings.*

Dipping Batter: Sift together 1 cup *sifted* GOLD MEDAL Flour, ½ tsp. salt, and 1 tsp. baking powder. Mix 1 egg, slightly beaten, ¼ cup vegetable oil, and 1 cup milk. Add to dry ingredients; beat with rotary beater until smooth.

Frying Tips:
1. Use dark heavy skillet or Dutch oven for frying.
2. Do not place a cover over oil while heating.
3. Cool fat before removing from skillet.

Peas Almondine in Foil

2 lb. fresh peas or 1 pkg.
  (12 oz.) frozen peas
⅓ cup sliced or slivered
  almonds

2 tbsp. butter
salt and pepper
1 pimiento, chopped, if
  desired

Place peas on single or double thickness of heavy-duty aluminum foil depending on method used for cooking. Cooking on briquets requires double thickness; cooking on grill requires only single thickness. Add almonds and butter. Sprinkle with salt and pepper. Wrap foil securely around food. Barbecue 18 to 20 min. on briquets or 30 to 35 min. on grill, turning once. Just before serving add pimiento. *6 servings.*

Mushrooms in Butter

Goes with steak like butter with bread.
Combine ½ lb. sliced or whole fresh mushrooms and 1½ tbsp. butter.
Wrap in foil; seal edges. Put on grill over hot coals. Cook 20 to 30 min.,
turning often. Serve with steak.

Outdoor Indian Pilaf

*An excellent accompaniment for beef... adapted from a famous dish of
exotic India. The rice develops a rich nutty flavor, so good when topped
with raisins and toasted almonds.*

⅓ cup butter
1 cup long grain rice,
    uncooked
1 clove garlic, minced

2½ to 3 cups beef bouillon
¼ cup raisins
2 tbsp. toasted slivered
    almonds

In heavy 9″ skillet, place butter, rice, and garlic. Sauté on outdoor
grill 4″ from briquets until rice turns orange. Remove from heat and
add bouillon. Cover with tight-fitting lid or aluminum foil which fits
securely around the edge of skillet. Simmer 45 to 50 min., or until
liquid is absorbed and rice is tender. (Check pilaf after 30 min. of
cooking and add more bouillon if needed.) Remove from heat, uncover,
sprinkle with raisins and almonds. Serve immediately. *4 servings.*

Note: Skillet must be tightly covered so that rice steams and fluffs
up while cooking.

Potatoes Roasted in the Coals

Few are the people who do not remember a glorious feast from child-hood—a rocky charred nubbin of potato raked from an empty lot or sea-shore fire. Many adults love to recapture this taste, and a delicious one it is. Choose medium to large potatoes for this method. If you are using a wood fire, bury potatoes in the ashes at the edge and rake hot coals over them. If using briquets, place potatoes right on them, turning fre-quently with tongs. After 45 to 60 min., crack off the charred casing and serve the mealy, smoke-flavored heart with lots of butter.

Potatoes Roasted in Foil

The most practical and rewarding way to cook potatoes on a grill. Pictured on page 140.

Rub skins of medium baking potatoes with oil or butter. Wrap each potato securely in heavy-duty aluminum foil. Roast directly on coals or on grill over coals depending on how meat is being prepared; turn often. Roast potatoes on coals 35 to 45 min., on grill about 1 hr., or until potatoes are soft when gently pressed with thumb in grilling mitts. Make crosswise slits through foil and potato. Fold foil back and squeeze until potato pops up through opening. Dot with butter; season with salt and pepper.

Potato Toppings: Set up a long tray with bowls of various toppings and let guests choose combinations of sour cream, chopped chives, chopped green onions and tops, minced parsley and green pepper, Par-mesan cheese or grated Swiss cheese, barbecue sauce, pats of butter, freshly ground black pepper, celery seeds, seasoned salt.

Roasted Sweet Potatoes

Sweet potatoes or yams are equally delicious roasted on the coals or in foil as directed above.

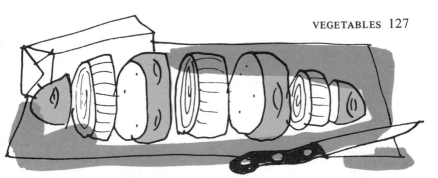

Roasted Potatoes and Onions

Peel baking potatoes. Cut in slices 1″ thick. Brush with butter and sprinkle with salt. Reassemble the potato with 1″ slices of onion between the slices of potato on a double thickness of aluminum foil. Drench the top with butter. Sprinkle with salt and pepper. Seal in foil and roast on coals about 45 min. Serve in foil.

Grilled Frozen Potato Products

Any of the many frozen potato products, such as French fries, shredded potato patties, rissoles, and potato puffs, are delicious cooked out of doors. Wrap in heavy-duty aluminum foil with 1 tbsp. butter and salt and pepper to taste. Grill 4 to 5″ above hot coals 20 to 25 min., turning once, until foil pkg. is soft to asbestos-gloved thumb.

Pan-fried Potatoes

Slice 6 raw or cooked medium potatoes about ⅛″ thick. Heap sliced potatoes lightly in 3 tbsp. butter, vegetable oil, or bacon drippings in skillet. Sprinkle layers with salt, pepper, and dried dill, if desired. Brown slowly until crispy, about 20 min. for cooked and about 30 min. for raw potatoes. Turn as sections brown. *6 servings.*

Skillet Scalloped or Au Gratin Potatoes

On a camping trip, you might prefer to use Betty Crocker Scalloped or Au Gratin Potatoes. Follow pkg. directions—except cook in a 9 or 10″ covered skillet over a slow fire. *4 to 6 servings.*

Cajun Fried Yams

Parboil 2 lb. sweet potatoes or yams. Cool. Peel and slice ¼″ thick. Place 2 tbsp. butter or bacon fat in bottom of 10″ skillet. Place just enough potatoes to cover bottom of skillet (do not overlap, place in single layer). Cook potatoes on both sides, 5 to 8 min. per side or until golden brown. Remove and sprinkle with granulated sugar. Repeat procedure with remaining potato slices. *4 to 6 servings.*

Sweet Potato and Pineapple Kabobs

Parboil sweet potatoes. Cool, remove peelings, and cut in cubes. Alternate on skewers with fresh or canned pineapple cubes. Brush with melted butter or bacon drippings. Grill over hot coals until browned, 20 to 30 min. Serve with grilled ham steak.

Variation: Wrap bacon strips around potatoes and secure with toothpick. Arrange on skewers as given in above directions.

Note: Canned sweet potatoes are too tender to skewer.

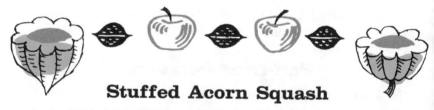

Stuffed Acorn Squash

Apple and brown sugar caramelize as squash bakes. Good with pork or baked turkey, as pictured on pages 34-35.

Select 3 medium acorn squash. Cut into halves; remove seeds. Place each half on a double thickness of heavy-duty aluminum foil. Put 1 tsp. butter and 2 tbsp. brown sugar in each half, add mixture of ¾ cup chopped apple and 2 tbsp. chopped walnuts. Dot with 2 tsp. butter and wrap securely in foil. Barbecue on briquets 40 to 50 min., or on grill about 1 hr., turning once. Squash is done when it feels soft when touched with an asbestos-gloved thumb. *6 servings.*

Acorn Squash with Honey-Chili Sauce

Grill acorn or Hubbard squash halves in foil as directed on page 128 with no filling and serve 1 tbsp. Honey-Chili Sauce (recipe below) in each.

Honey-Chili Sauce

½ cup butter, melted
½ cup honey
3 tbsp. sweet chow chow
1 tbsp. chili powder

1 clove garlic, crushed
1 tsp.salt
⅛ tsp. pepper
⅛ tsp. nutmeg

Mix all ingredients; serve warm or cold. *Makes about 1 cup.*

Foil-grilled Zucchini

A sure way to delight zucchini lovers.

Slice zucchini crosswise in ¼″ slices. Place portions (one per person) on double thickness of heavy-duty aluminum foil. Sprinkle each with salt, coarse freshly ground black pepper, grated Parmesan cheese, and 1 tbsp. water; dot with 2 tsp. butter. Wrap foil securely. Cook on briquets about 15 min., or on grill about 20 min., turning once.

Canned Vegetables Campfire Style

Remove labels from cans. Cut almost around the top, leaving top in place for a lid and heat on the grill. (Do not put an unopened can on the fire. It may explode.) When hot, drain, add butter and seasonings. A good way to deal with baby beets, boiled new potatoes, or whole onions.

SALADS

Salads, of course, are a welcome addition to outdoor eating. What better complement for a sizzling steak than a tangy tossed green salad! And fried chicken just isn't a picnic without a creamy potato salad chockfull of hard-cooked egg, celery, and radishes. Teens will love colorful tomato relish on their hamburgers. And you must try the exciting variations on a theme of de luxe deviled eggs.

Tossed Salad with Cauliflowerets

1 medium head lettuce
1 small head cauliflower
1 small, sweet Bermuda onion
1 medium green pepper, diced
1 pimiento, diced (about 3 tbsp.)
6 large fresh mushrooms, washed and thinly sliced (about 1 cup)

½ cup pitted green olives, sliced
½ cup Roquefort cheese, crumbled
1 clove garlic, crushed or grated
Classic French Dressing (recipe below)

Tear lettuce into bite-size pieces. Wash cauliflower and remove green stalks. Separate into tiny flowerets. Cut onion in paper-thin rings. Toss gently with green pepper, pimiento, mushrooms, olives, and cheese. Chill about 1 hr. Toss and serve immediately with Classic French Dressing. *6 to 8 servings.*

Classic French Dressing: Mix 2 tbsp. vegetable oil, 2 tbsp. white wine (tarragon) vinegar, 1 clove garlic, pressed and minced, 1½ tsp. salt, dash of freshly ground pepper, and dash of flavor enhancer (monosodium glutamate).

Note: For crisp greens and vegetables, keep cool in foil or in an insulated container. Toss with dressing when ready to serve.

Potato Salad

A summer picnic favorite, pictured on page 33.

4 cups cubed cooked potatoes
¼ cup clear French dressing
   (or ¼ cup vegetable oil
   and 2 tbsp. vinegar)
3 hard-cooked eggs, cut up

1 cup diced celery
2 to 3 tbsp. chopped onion
½ cup salad dressing or
   mayonnaise

Marinate potatoes in French dressing for 1 to 2 hr. Add remaining ingredients; season with salt and pepper. Serve in lettuce-lined bowl; garnish with 1 hard-cooked egg, parsley, and pimiento. *6 servings.*

Good 'N Easy Potato Salad

1 pkg. Betty Crocker
   Scalloped Potatoes
3 cups water
2 tbsp. butter

⅔ cup water
¼ cup mayonnaise
1 tsp. prepared mustard
2 hard-cooked eggs, chopped

Empty potatoes into saucepan. Add 3 cups water. Bring to boil. Reduce heat and simmer until tender, about 15 min. Rinse with cold water; drain thoroughly. Put in bowl, cover, and chill. Melt butter. Blend in contents of seasoning pkg. Add ⅔ cup water all at once. Heat over medium heat until mixture boils, stirring constantly. Cover and chill. (Lumps are onion pieces.) When cold, blend mayonnaise and mustard into sauce. Fold into potatoes and eggs. *4 servings.*

Potato Salad for a Crowd

5 lb. potatoes (2½ qt. cooked
   and diced)
½ cup French dressing
4 hard-cooked eggs, diced

6 tbsp. finely chopped green
   pepper
½ cup finely chopped
   pimiento
3 cups thinly sliced celery
¼ cup minced onion

Cook potatoes in skins; peel and dice. While warm, marinate with French dressing. Add eggs, green pepper, pimiento, celery, and onion. Add Dressing (recipe below). Mix lightly just until blended. Chill thoroughly. *25 servings.*

Dressing: Blend 2 cups mayonnaise, ¼ cup prepared mustard, 1½ tsp. paprika, 2 tbsp. salt, and 1 tsp. white pepper.

Note: Be sure to keep all salads made with mayonnaise or salad dressing well chilled. Do not serve a second day.

Summer Macaroni Salad

A quick and colorful macaroni salad to serve with a main dish.

1 pkg. (7 or 8 oz.) elbow, shell,
   or ring macaroni
1 cup cubed Cheddar cheese
1 cup sliced gherkins

½ cup minced onion
½ cup mayonnaise
1 pkg. (10 or 12 oz.) frozen
   peas, cooked and drained

Cook macaroni according to pkg. directions. Add cheese, gherkins, onion, mayonnaise to cooled macaroni and peas. Season with salt and pepper to taste. Chill before serving. Serve on bed of lettuce. *About 4 cups.*

Mexican Green Bean Salad

Marinate 2 cups cooked thinly sliced fresh or frozen French green beans in 2 or 3 tbsp. French dressing with 2 tbsp. minced onion several hr. or overnight. Add 2 to 3 tbsp. grated sharp cheese. Garnish with red or white onion rings. *4 servings.*

Zucchini Tossed Salad

½ head lettuce, torn into bite-size pieces
½ head romaine, torn into bite-size pieces
2 medium zucchini, thinly sliced
1 cup sliced radishes
3 green onions, sliced (about 2 tbsp.)
1 oz. Bleu cheese, crumbled (about 2 tbsp.)
vegetable oil
Classic Garlic Dressing

Toss lettuce, romaine, zucchini, radishes, onions, and cheese with vegetable oil just until leaves glisten. Then toss with Classic Garlic Dressing (recipe below). *6 servings.*

Classic Garlic Dressing: Combine and mix well 2 tbsp. tarragon vinegar, 1½ tsp. salt, 1 clove garlic, crushed, dash of ground black pepper, and dash of flavor enhancer (monosodium glutamate).

Note: For easy slicing of zucchini, use vegetable slicer or peeler.

Caesar Salad

Place 3 qt. salad greens in large bowl. Add ⅓ cup *each* vegetable oil, grated dry cheese, and crumbled Bleu cheese. Salt and pepper to taste. Break one raw egg over greens. Squeeze juice from 2 lemons over egg. Toss well. Dribble 2 tbsp. oil with garlic steeped in it over 1 pt. crisp croutons (bread cubes browned); add just before serving. *8 servings.*

Beet Salad with Caraway French Dressing

Bright red and green—lends zip to any outdoor dinner.

1 can (1 lb. 4 oz.) beets
  (chunks or whole) or
  cooked fresh beets
2 tsp. caraway seeds, if
  desired

1 cup Classic French Dressing
  (recipe p. 130)
1 bunch curly endive

Slice beets thinly. Mix caraway seeds with French dressing. Pour dressing over beets and let stand 1 hr. before serving. Chop endive coarsely and toss with drained beets. Serve immediately. *6 servings.*

Peanut Crunch Slaw

Luscious cole slaw with creamy dressing and added crunch from "cheesed" peanuts.

4 cups shredded cabbage
1 cup finely cut celery
½ cup commercial sour cream
½ cup mayonnaise
1 tsp. salt
¼ cup chopped green onions

¼ cup chopped green pepper
½ cup chopped cucumber
1 tbsp. butter
½ cup salted peanuts,
  coarsely chopped
2 tbsp. Parmesan cheese

Toss cabbage and celery together. Chill. Mix sour cream, mayonnaise, salt, onions, green pepper, and cucumber; chill. In small skillet, melt butter; add peanuts and heat until lightly browned. Immediately stir in cheese. Just before serving, toss chilled vegetables with dressing. Sprinkle peanuts on top. *6 to 8 servings.*

Note: If time is short, eliminate the final three ingredients and sprinkle chopped salted peanuts over salad.

Tomatoes Vinaigrette

Wonderful with roast beef and baked potatoes. as pictured on pages 140-141.

Arrange in 8 or 9″ sq. pan 8 or 9 thick tomato slices or smaller whole tomatoes (with tops cut off). Spoon over tomatoes mixture of: 2 cloves garlic (pressed or minced), 1 tsp. salt, ½ tsp. pepper, 2 tsp. oregano, ½ tsp. dry mustard, ⅓ cup wine vinegar, and 1 cup olive or vegetable oil. Cover. Refrigerate 2 to 3 hr., basting occasionally. To serve, sprinkle with minced onion and parsley and some of dressing. *8 servings.*

Satellite Tomatoes

Individual salads for young space enthusiasts. Pictured on page 138.

Prepare small carrot and celery sticks and green onions the same length, about 3½″. Wash medium-sized tomatoes (peel, if desired). To make satellites, remove tomato core. Make two small slashes in each tomato, about ½″ long, on either side of hole where core was removed. Insert a carrot stick and celery stick. Insert onion in center of each tomato. Serve as individual salads at outdoor picnic. Take tomatoes and vegetable sticks along on picnic, assemble there.

Summertime Tomato Relish

Excellent hot or cold—with fried chicken or hamburgers.

3 lb. peeled tomatoes, diced	1 tsp. sugar
3 green peppers, diced	¼ cup vegetable oil
3 medium onions, chopped	¼ cup vinegar
1 tsp. salt	½ tsp. dry mustard
¼ tsp. pepper	

Cook first 6 ingredients in oil gently, stirring occasionally, 3 min. or until vegetables are slightly softened. Add vinegar and mustard. Store in jars and chill well. Serve at picnic cold or reheated. *6 servings.*

Tuna Stuffed Eggs and Variations

6 hard-cooked eggs
1 can (6½ oz.) flaked tuna,
   with liquid
2 tsp. prepared mustard
1½ tsp. Worcestershire sauce

2 tsp. lemon juice
¼ tsp. salt
⅛ tsp. pepper
¼ cup mayonnaise

Halve eggs lengthwise and remove yolks. Press yolks through a sieve or crumble finely with a fork; mix with rest of ingredients. With fork or small spatula, lightly pile filling in white halves. Garnish with parsley. Sprinkle with paprika for more color.

Curried Tuna Stuffed Eggs: Follow recipe above—*except* add ⅛ tsp. curry powder to mixture.

Deviled Eggs with Sour Cream: Omit tuna and mayonnaise in above recipe and moisten with ½ cup thick commercial sour cream.

Shrimp Stuffed Eggs: Follow recipe above—*except* substitute 1 can (4½ oz.) shrimp, chopped, for tuna.

Bacon Stuffed Eggs: Follow recipe above—*except* substitute ¼ lb. crisp, cooked bacon (about 8 slices), crumbled, for tuna.

Double Deviled Eggs: Follow recipe above—*except* substitute 1 can (2¼ oz.) deviled ham for tuna.

Stuffed Eggs Au Gratin: Follow recipe above—*except* substitute ⅔ cup shredded sharp Cheddar cheese for tuna. Increase mayonnaise 2 tbsp.

Salmon Stuffed Eggs: Follow recipe above—*except* substitute 1 can (8 oz.) salmon with juice for tuna. *(Note:* Remove skin and small bones in salmon before adding to egg yolks.)